HOW NOT TO GET SCREWED BY YOUR LAWYER

HOW NOT TO GET SCREWED BY YOUR LAWYER

A SYSTEM FOR BUSINESS OWNERS
TO MANAGE COSTS, REDUCE STRESS
& TAKE BACK CONTROL

DANIELA LISCIO

First Print Edition, June 2022.

Published by the Author.

LIONCREST
PUBLISHING

COPYRIGHT © 2022 EAT FOR SPORT LLC

All rights reserved.

HOW NOT TO GET SCREWED BY YOUR LAWYER
A System for Business Owners to Manage Costs, Reduce Stress & Take Back Control

ISBN   978-1-5445-2988-2   *Hardcover*

       978-1-5445-2987-5   *Paperback*

       978-1-5445-2986-8   *Ebook*

CONTENTS

Mom and Dad,
thanks for letting me be me...
or at least putting up with me being me.
I love you.

FOOTNOTES

IF YOU'D LIKE TO DISCUSS ANY OF THE REFERENCES, notes, and additional commentary in the footnotes, or comment on them with agreement or disagreement, love or vitriol, or if you'd like to challenge any of the references or ideas, please email me at daniela@danielaliscio.com. Additional commentary, updated references and/or corrections to mistakes can be found by visiting manageyourlawyer.com/bonus, or by scanning the QR code below.

INTRODUCTION

BECAUSE WE ALL PUT OUR PANTS ON THE SAME WAY

"MY EX'S LAWYER IS SUING ME," CAME THE INCREDULOUS voice on the other end of the phone.

The conflict-infected arrangement had started in a lawyer's office with both divorcing wife and husband, and complications arose shortly thereafter. The lawyer—who may or may not have passed his cognitive prime—ended up suing the husband for a slight that should not, in a sane world, have ever been actionable.

But I shouldn't start this book by saying such dumb things. Of course, nearly everything is "actionable." And who can adequately define "sane"?

Regardless, it was one of many little-guy problems that I saw less frequently in my prior life but now, I had a front-row seat.

Just a couple of years earlier, I had left my New York City lawyering life and partnership after meeting the love of my life on the way down from the summit of Mount Kilimanjaro. What a cliché, I know. Still, it's slightly more interesting than if we'd hooked up in a bar, even if the results were no less up in the air.

Cringy career change notwithstanding, the business world had been beckoning for years. Following two degrees in economics and some boring corporate-world experience, my early fascination with Perry Mason wasn't shaking loose and law school was still etched in my brain. I stopped fighting it and off I went. But unlike the dapper Perry, I was interested in corporate law from the very beginning. There was nothing in criminals, family hardship, or litigation for me.

The university I attended for law school had a strong business school, and despite having absolutely no intention of getting an MBA along with a law degree when I first arrived, I left four years later with both. At that time, I still believed more education would give me more options.

I realized only later the opposite might be true in more ways than meets the eyeballs. That's a different book.

Upon graduation, students with combined law and MBA degrees have to decide whether they'll head into business or law. I chose corporate law and stayed with the same firm for twelve years. Except like all good things—while I enjoyed law, genuinely liked most of my clients, and appreciated the constant learning—it was time to grow up, get out of the altitude, and off the mountain.

Into business I went, where the air may not have been clearer but was definitely more oxygen-rich. There I breathed the long, deep breaths of highs and lows, successes and failures, learnings and unlearnings, alongside the constant thrill of creativity and shiny newness that business demands.

Traveling new roads littered with caravans of other business owners and entrepreneurs, weathered and battle-scarred but still as bright-eyed as small business required, the law looked different.

I got to see the law the way it was for regular folk. Outside the safe bubble of big corporate law and big clients with legal teams or in-house counsel, it *was* different.

The problems were vast and expansive. In addition to the more obscure legal situations I'd get wind of (like lawyers suing clients), there were obvious challenges—things like trying to find a lawyer with the right expertise, struggling through communication hiccups with an existing lawyer, or just the usual delays in justice.

But there were more surprising and insidious issues, too. Those were far more unique to the little guy.

Despite the billions of dollars spent on legal services, I saw too many of these regular people and small business clients feeling alone on the battlefield, like their own lawyer wasn't even on their team. It wasn't only that some felt intimidated, through no real fault of their lawyers. It was that many felt violated. And that was, at least in part, the fault of their lawyers.

And themselves.

There's nothing easy about managing people. And yet, disciplines like organizational behavior are often scoffed at or simply given lip service—which is what might explain a gazillion books written on such topics only to have to read the same regurgitated dogma over and over.

I certainly recall my business school colleagues sneering at having to take a class in management behavior. I sneered alongside them. We wanted the tangible stuff—finance, operations, and accounting.

Management behavior sounded like horseshit.

Except, as anyone with even a little life experience can attest, managing people is the hardest business function on the planet. Right after getting all the words out to order a grande pumpkin spice frap with oat milk and one-third decaf, no whip.

Here's where we go wrong when it comes to working with a lawyer. We hire them for their expertise, and then it's hands off. We become kind of like my dogs when they roll over on their backs for a belly rub—submissive. *Do what you will with me!* But not in a good way.

Until now. Until you finish this book. Because when you finish this book, you'll never return to that approach again. The world needs alphas.

Inside these pages you will learn:

- The inherent difficulties in the legal landscape and how to maneuver them like cones around a racetrack.

- How to systemize your legal process to make it easier to follow through with the steps you'll learn in this book.

- How to improve communications, no matter how bad your lawyer's bedside manner (or yours).

- How to protect your money and keep it in your and your business's pocket and out of your lawyer's pinstripe silk lining.

- How to reach within yourself and draw on your existing skills to manage the legal process and your lawyer effectively (because Tony Robbins says we're either growing or we're dying, and he's probably right).

- The glorious evolution of alternatives to traditional law firms and how to use them.

- How to create a team dynamic with your lawyer that is productive and—just maybe, if you can keep a smile on your face, perseverance in your heart, and lightness in your soul—fun.

Once you learn these things, rolling over will be for suckers. Not for you.

And if you're thinking you already know that you need to be proactive, well, even though many of us know we shouldn't be rollover dogs, we don't execute. We know we should have a green smoothie in the morning, too, but we go for the bacon. It's just so salty and we must have bacon!

Humans have a knack for doing things we shouldn't and not doing things we should. So even when we're ahead of the curve and *recognize* that we shouldn't completely take a back seat, we do just that. And we justify it with:

- "I'm too busy."

- "That's what I'm paying them for!"

- "It's their job, not mine."

- "I'd rather pull my fingernails out than have to deal with the stress of calling that a—hole again."

But even the "best" excuse for why we choose the bacon over the green smoothie doesn't make it the best option. The reality is that being proactive is at the heart of any happy legal relationship. I don't know that drinking green smoothies, working out, and limiting alcohol (shucks) are going to keep me healthy or help me live longer, and I still may get a chronic disease that will kill me. But my chances are better with them, and they are all within my control.

And just like many other bad habits we aim to correct, we can change our patterns and behaviors to make our responses more

proactive and lessen the chance that some douchebag lawyer—
or even some nice lawyer—will take advantage of us.

They still may, just like any one person can purposely or inad-
vertently take advantage of another person. We can't escape that
reality. It's just that being proactive ensures we're able to stand as
strong as that hot warrior who tells the metrosexual giant during
the Battle of Thermopylae while the Persian Empire knocked on
Greece's gates, "Kneeling will be hard for me."

I wrote this book because clients have bent the knee for too long
with no reward. Traditional legal services have not asked in a
productive way, "How do we better help the end user of legal
services?" Other than the ragtag collection of freebie articles that
law firms scatter on their boring websites to help generate clients,
the advice people get to prepare them for the inevitable frustra-
tions between lawyer and client is disappointing and insufficient.

More significantly, clients need to know their lawyers have
their back and that they believe in them more than they believe
in themselves. Instead, most clients end up frustrated in a
confusing and convoluted system, feeling alone and without
control over their legal situation.

No more.

This book will empower legal services users in a way that has—
until now—been disregarded.

Although it would be impossible to fix the problems in the
legal system and take away the headaches it will cause you, it *is*

possible to improve your relationship with your lawyer so that you do your part to reduce your legal bill, protect your assets, avoid unnecessary stress,[1] potentially improve the direction of your legal matter, and develop a productive and engaged partnership with your attorney.

These pages are not filled with deep, dark secrets that take a rocket scientist to figure out. Rather, they provide a simple and accessible process that anyone can apply.

All it takes is a proactive and sleuthing mentality and the decision to embrace your role in the relationship with your lawyer as the *team owner*. That job is not your lawyer's. It's yours. You're the one who pays the bills, endures the consequences, and enjoys the fruits. Your lawyer may be the quarterback, or maybe even the coach. But you are the team owner, so it's your *obligation* to be Leonidas. It's your obligation to help your lawyer achieve the best win for you.

---

1 Kelly McGonigal, "How to Make Stress Your Friend," June 2013, https://www.ted.com/talks/kelly_mcgonigal_how_to_make_stress_your_friend.

McGonigal, a health psychologist and lecturer at Stanford University, delivered this widely viewed TED Talk. The nuts and bolts are that your attitude toward stress contributes to how your body physiologically responds to it. If you believe that stress is your body's natural ability to help you deal with things that happen in life, your body will not stress out, including with the consequential responses that increase risk of heart disease. If you believe stress is bad, your body will respond in a way that increases your risk of heart disease. Implementing the steps in this book lends itself to viewing stress as a controllable force that is not bad; rather, it is something that can be controlled and dealt with through proactive effort. As a result, there is a huge opening for you to see your lawyer in the same way; making your lawyer a "friend" could be good for you.

The payoff is you'll learn to better manage your lawyer with the fortunate side effect of learning how to better manage every professional relationship in your life. Maybe even the personal ones, too.

With your permission, let's begin.

CHAPTER 1

HOUSE LANNISTER GOT NOTHIN' ON THE LEGAL SYSTEM

TYRION LANNISTER SUFFERED DADDY ISSUES ALL HIS LIFE and then, late one night in medieval Westeros, after an already stressful ordeal involving a fraudulent legal proceeding and a death sentence, discovered that his father was bedding his ex-lover. The camel's back was broken. Tyrion wound his way through dim castle corridors lit with twinkling torches searching for his father, anger and betrayal racing through his heart. He found him sitting on the pot. Tyrion raised his massive crossbow and shot his father. Twice. Dead as a doornail.

Surely, that must be one of the worst ways to die.

That small slice of family dysfunction in the entire *Game of Thrones* pie is nothing compared to the dysfunction in the justice system. It's a dysfunctional mess no matter what side of the political seesaw you sit on.

For example:

- Solutions for legitimate problems sacrificed in favor of political points.

- Conflicting and confusing laws.

- Conflicting case law, sometimes the result of biased judges or human error.

- The legal profession scapegoating other industries and professions to avoid searching into its own dark soul.

- Regulatory bodies defying their own rules and the rule of law.

Perhaps we're addicted to dysfunction because it provides a clue into our own. I don't know. We are emotional, irrational creatures made more irrational by the belief that we are cool-headed and rational.

Legal migraines will always exist and this book isn't intended to be the Excedrin®.[2] The legal system's problems can't be fixed in one mere book. Maybe they could. But this isn't it.

---

2 For legal migraines to improve, we need an objective examination of the legal system's failures. Those failures include at least these two issues: we need to get politics out of prosecuting attorneys, and we need to eliminate the two-tier justice system where one applies to upper echelons of society and the other to the proletariat. We shouldn't hold our breath waiting for either, which will ensure legal headaches continue.

Luckily, one of the shining lights in anyone's life is to focus on what is within our control rather than what isn't. It's a simple beacon for a better life. We'll do no differently here. In this chapter, we'll look at a few places where those beacons shine to better appreciate the legal landscape and more clearly articulate what we can control and what we cannot.

A NEW ZEITGEIST

We've arrived at a new place. Among our shared disappointment with the education system, consistently poor predictions of mind-boggling proportions by "experts," and the shockingly homogeneous groupthink of the intelligentsia, we've started to ask with more gusto, *What does it mean to be smart?*

We all know there's a difference between IQ and EQ and every other acronym in between that measures the sum of an individual. Yet, we have assumed that a person is smarter because of the nature of their studies, that a person with a law degree is somehow more intelligent than a person without. Maybe it extends to all professional degrees like accounting, medicine, engineering, certain sciences, and teaching.

Why?

Is the professor teaching your kids in college the person you'd choose to maneuver your company's greatest operational challenge? Is that teacher the one you'd choose as a survivor buddy if stranded on a deserted island?

Do those smart and pedigreed lawyers and doctors not get into financial pickles? Do they never get divorced, have shitty kids, or get into work conundrums and squabbles with their colleagues?

Do they always avoid bad buying or investment decisions? Do law firms manage themselves better than other businesses? Do those with the degrees make better leaders after we strip away the $500 shoes and -isms upon which they make their commercials and websites and fund their white papers?

If ever there were rhetorical questions.

Plus, the American Bar Association reports that lawyers have a higher incidence of suicides, mental illness, and substance abuse than the general populace.

A 2016 study concluded that "attorneys experience problematic drinking that is hazardous, harmful, or otherwise consistent with alcohol use disorders at a higher rate than other professional populations."[3] It also mentioned that "depression, anxiety, and stress are also significant problems for this population and most notably associated with the same personal and professional characteristics."

---

3 Patrick R. Krill, Ryan Johnson, and Linda Albert, "The Prevalence of Substance Use and Other Mental Health Concerns among American Attorneys," *Journal of Addiction Medicine*, January–February, 2016, https://pubmed.ncbi.nlm.nih.gov/26825268/. A 2016 study by the American Bar Association Commission on Lawyer Assistance, in conjunction with the Hazelden Betty Ford Foundation.

Whether this is because the profession attracts or creates these problems, in a licensed profession with its messy fingers all over significant aspects of policy, education, and politics...

...that's kind of a big deal.

There's much nuttiness in life, and it doesn't pass over law firms because they've slathered their doors with the blood, sweat, and tears of their lawyers and pinned up copies of law degrees.

All this is to say that our idea of "smart" is finally correcting course. It's not all about qualifications. Intelligence is important to analyzing complex legal problems and manifesting them into precise documentation, building a bridge, or developing a vaccine.

But it's inescapable that many other factors go into "smartness."

It includes our ability to:

- Weed out confirmation bias and unravel the complicated business of cognitive dissonance that keeps all of us locked in our own mental prisons.

- Decipher the humanistic qualities that connect us to another human soul.

- Teach.

- Communicate disagreement and emotion-laden topics.

- Empathize.

- Show gumption, tenacity, and learning from past behavior in the face of repeated failure and hardship.

- Solve problems by the sum of our experience regardless of education or training.

- Take the advice of Steve Jobs and not be trapped by dogma along with having the courage to follow our hearts.[4]

The next zeitgeist will display an even greater understanding of this, if it hasn't already.

INCENTIVES

Lawyers—despite being wonkier than the average citizen, according to the ABA—are critically important to the justice equation. They are involved in every aspect of it.

They also act within a system that incentivizes them in ways that conflict with improving justice and putting service to the client first. A large proportion of lawyers have their clients' best interests in mind, but they are also incentivized in the wrong places.

---

4 Steve Jobs, CEO of Apple and Pixar Entertainment, Stanford University commencement address, June 12, 2005, video, https://www.youtube.com/watch?v=UF8uR6Z6KLc. Jobs stated, "Don't be trapped by dogma, which is living with the results of other people's thinking...and most important, have the courage to follow your heart and intuition; they somehow already know what you truly want to become. Everything else is secondary."

These two things are both true.

Lawyers make money when people have more legal problems and when those problems last longer. They benefit financially when regulations and laws are complicated, conflicting, and confusing.

Although money doesn't frame all intentions, it sure does make the world go round. Lawyers have families and desires, too. They want their kids in the best schools. They want travel and prestige. And it's a tough job. Do they really have the bandwidth to make "the system" better while they're trying to survive a strenuous, demanding, and constantly evolving job?

Moreover, there is much disagreement about where the problems in the industry lie. Lawyers are just a cog in an unfair wheel, and it's much simpler to say, "What can I do?" and "It's not my fault."

The wheels of justice turn slowly, we're told. But those who can make them turn at all, let alone more quickly, aren't incentivized to do it.

Who is? Judges? Judges sit on their perch under a guise of impartiality, have their quota of cases and causes to support in between trips to their country clubs, and otherwise stand within the walls of protected justice and the same excuses lawyers rely on.

No matter how much a politician wants to throw money at a problem to deny the nature of incentives in our lives, incentives matter. And nothing in the legal system will be fixed while it clings to its systemic misunderstanding of incentives in a human being's life.

This sounds impossible to overcome. It isn't. There's a good chance that innovation and evolution, although sometimes as slow-moving as those giant tortoises in the Galapagos, will take down any industry that favors the service provider over the one who needs the service. There's no reason to believe the legal industry may not face the same fate. In the meantime, new brands of legal services have indeed risen with the growth of alternative legal service providers (ALSPs). ALSPs at least claim to realign incentive structures to put the client first and deliver legal services more effectively. We'll discuss ALSPs more in Chapter 9.

PERCEPTIONS

The first thing we do, let's kill all the lawyers.

Shakespeare wrote it in *Henry VI* in the seventeenth century. It could as easily be written today.[5]

---

5   William Shakespeare, *Henry VI, Part 2*. There is more to the phrase than meets the eye. (See, for example, the discussion in Jonathan Healy, "The First Thing We Do, Let's Kill All the Lawyers," The Social Historian, August 25, 2015, https://thesocialhistorian.wordpress.com/2015/08/25/the-first-thing-we-do-lets-kill-all-the-lawyers/.)

Nonetheless, in common day parlance, it captures a distaste for lawyers that is consistently revealed in surveys regarding the public's perception of lawyers. For example, a 2020 Pew Research study reveals only 44 percent of the public believes lawyers adhere to high or very high ethical standards.

Jeffery Gottfried, Mason Walker, and Amy Mitchell, "Americans Are More Negative in Their Broader Views of Journalists than They Are toward COVID-19," Pew Research Center, May 8, 2020, https://www.pewresearch.org/

Less than one in five people think lawyers contribute a lot to society.[6] And the factors that play into those feels are not improving, so it's unlikely that the perception of lawyers will change anytime soon.

It's partly that lawyers are associated with a problem—some legal challenge that's complicated or stressful or expensive. It's partly that the justice system is convoluted and challenging, and the lawyer is the portal through which we navigate that system. It's partly that it's hard to get through life without needing a lawyer, and we often rebel against things we need but would rather not have to deal with.

None of that is enough of an explanation. We could make the same argument about doctors, for example. Doctors are also associated with problems we don't want to deal with. The medical system is challenging and expensive, and we need doctors to help us wade through it. Yet, we don't generally think of doctors as a scourge upon humanity, even if most of us have probably had a negative experience with a doctor (and even if the COVID-19 pandemic has, at least arguably, impacted the public's trust in the medical profession).

---

journalism/2020/05/08/americans-are-more-negative-in-their-broader-views-of-journalists-than-they-are-toward-covid-19-coverage/.

6 "Public Esteem for Military Still High," Pew Research Center, July 11, 2013, https://www.pewforum.org/2013/07/11/public-esteem-for-military-still-high/. True, the Pew study reveals that about 43 percent of the public say lawyers make "some" contribution to society.

On first blush, that sounds more promising than the one in five who think lawyers contribute "a lot." But one must wonder what the public would say to the same question about any profession. (If I was asked, "Do you think hairdressers/plumbers/baristas/etc. make 'some' contribution to society?" The answer for me, and I'll bet a lot of others, perhaps even at least 43 percent worth, would be a resounding yes.) So maybe it's not as promising as that first blush.

It may be nothing more than people feel good about their lawyers when they get a result that is worth the time and effort expended. Otherwise, no matter how good the lawyer or the legal work, if the client's result stinks, the lawyer is more likely to be classified as a reptile. I'll never forget watching a friend's pain melt away at the end of a five-year torturous litigation when she won her case.

For whatever reason the negative perception of lawyers exists, right or wrong as it may be, such a level of distrust makes things not right with the world. It sounds trite, but doesn't the ability of an industry to provide the best service demand a level of trust better than what the legal industry has achieved in the last 500 years?[7]

It puts in stark contrast the nurtured and mutually respected relationship of a lawyer and a happy client. To be fair to lawyers (and indeed the very reason for this book), clients have some role in this equation and can do their part to work to change the perception. It's not helpful to say, "All lawyers suck." It's much more productive to achieve a position that lets you say, "Even though most lawyers suck, my lawyer is a trusted advisor and we have a great relationship. My lawyer is part of my team." Accomplishing that mutually respected relationship has the scope to dim the otherwise difficult parts of the profession.

---

7 Some authors suggest the reputation of our ancient lawyers took a hit somewhere in the Middle Ages, the fifth century through the Renaissance.

BUSINESSPEOPLE ARE MASOCHISTS, THANK THE HEAVENS

How else do you explain the constant effort that leads to embarrassment and failure? "Business is the greatest personal development journey you can go on," Tony Robbins says.[8] It's an insightful comment. Any businessperson can tell you how important it is to learn how to adjust and move on after making mistakes or falling flat on your face and looking like a chump.

It's the business world that ultimately solves most of the world's problems. And maybe that's because of the businessperson's flirtation with and masochistic need for failing, learning, and moving on.

There is arguably nothing more inspiring than the ability for people to just do it—the quest for growth, depth, debauchery, and better judgment in the name of finding solutions to a consumer's health, wealth, or relationship problems. Honing into better instincts in order to persevere.

This is very much the human experience. Those who succeed—no matter how success is measured—are those who know how to *recover better than anyone else*. From athletics to research to writing, to all forms of art to emotional intelligence to intellectual robustness, it's there and it's real.

Unfortunately, I mostly suck at it.

---

8 Tony Robbins, Business Mastery live event, speech, Las Vegas, August 2019.

Fortunately, it's a learned skill, and in the course of being a businessperson, you just get better at the perseverance mindset. You have to.

If you're surviving, that means you've got enough of that healthy mindset that will ensure you address any less-than-satisfactory relationship with your lawyer head-on and put the information in this book to good use. Small adjustments make for dramatic changes in results.

In case your eyes are rolling around in their sockets at the mention of mindset, not to worry! This book isn't going to delve into a bunch of personal development stuff because I'm certainly not the one to give it to you. And it's exhausting. The only thing I'd like you to appreciate is that a growth mindset in this case only demands that you leave a window open for the winds of change to blow in. And those winds of change are here for the shift in seeing yourself as your lawyer's lackey to the team owner.

It's a yes-no decision, so it's the easiest one you'll make all day.

SYSTEM SUGGESTIONS

In the following chapters, I'll provide a few suggestions to help you develop a system for proactively dealing with your lawyer rather than playing along as a casual observer. You'll still need to build out the other steps that help you get done what needs to get done, based on your unique circumstances. If it's helpful to think of the suggestions as a framework instead of a system, to bend, mold, and maneuver the material in this book, that's great too.

The pertinent part is to remember that the legal industry's dysfunction does not give you a *get-out-of-jail-free card* that keeps you from focusing on what you *can* control to improve the relationship with your lawyer to make it work better for you.

You have an important part to play in creating a mutually rewarding relationship. As a businessperson, you already have a head start on adopting the growth mindset necessary to ensure you don't get screwed *and* you contribute to the effort that makes your lawyer a true agent working in your interest.

CHAPTER 2

GOALS ARE FOR LOSERS

IT'S SHOCKING HOW MUCH BETTER LIFE IS WITH A DAILY green smoothie. My favorite combination is a mix of hearty greens, half a celery stalk, a one-inch piece of cucumber, three-quarters of a cup of chopped pineapple, a lemon, and a chunk of ginger root.

(Bet you didn't think you would find a recipe in this book, let alone one that could change your life.)

I like to pick greens out of my garden when I walk my dogs in the morning. At the end of the summer, I process those greens into green ice cubes with my Vitamix® for when it's not garden season in the Ozarks. Part of my put-the-groceries-away process is to peel and cut up chunks of ginger and lemon and wash cucumber and celery before putting them in stay-fresh containers. All that makes the green smoothie thing in the morning a no-brainer. Done almost by rote.

My goal is to have a green smoothie every day. The steps and processes required to make that happen are the green smoothie system. For travel days, I do something different. My green smoothie system rarely fails.

The pieces that feel incomplete on their own but are integral to getting across the bridge, to that pot at the end of the rainbow, *to the goal*, are the system. Scott Adams, creator of the *Dilbert* cartoon, author, and political commentator, popularized the concept of "systems over goals" in his book *How to Fail at Almost Anything and Still Win Big.*[9] As he says, "Goals are for losers." Almost self-explanatory.

A goal does not a habit make,[10] and without a system, a goal is a dream that will stay in never-never land. It's the difference between the three-times-a-week types[11] and the get-in-the-

---

9 Scott Adams, *How To Fail at Almost Anything and Still Win Big* (London: Penguin Portfolio, 2013). Parents might be wise to forgo college tuition and instead have their kids study this book. In fact, I am seriously considering offering my nieces money to read Adams's book, along with completing projects I assign them. throughout, rather than contributing to their university education. (Warning: I do not have children; do not take advice on children from someone without them.)

10 James Clear, *Atomic Habits* (New York: Penguin Random House, 2018); Charles Duhigg, *The Power of Habit* (New York City: Random House, 2012). Both authors do a wonderful job of discussing habits.

11 "Trending Topic: Physical Activity Guidelines," American College of Sports Medicine, March 16, 2022, https://www.acsm.org/read-research/trending-topics-resource-pages/physical-activity-guidelines/lists/guidelines-resources/physical-activity-guidelines-for-americans-2nd-edition.

Three times a week, the oft-seen recommended exercise frequency, usually fails, along with the rest of the advice dumbed down for the masses in the race to the lowest common denominator that continues, unabated and with breathless fervor. In this case, it likely emerged from more fulsome recommendations from the American College of Sports Medicine, which recommends moderate-intensity aerobic exercise three to five days a week or vigorous aerobic exercise for at least twenty minutes three days a week, as well as activities to maintain or improve muscular or

gym-every-morning-no-matter-what types. The former have a higher probability of waking up on Saturday, bemoaning the fact that there are only two days left in a week of zero gym attendance. It is the nagging in the back of your mind that you must get to the gym but haven't made it happen before the week is over. Another opportunity to say, "Ah well, I'll start again Monday."

Conversely, those in the gym every morning are out of bed when the alarm goes off. Their workout clothes and everything they need to execute on their day is ready to go. They don't like exercising any more than anyone else. They don't have any more willpower than anyone else. Instead, they have put together systems that allow them to execute on the things they need to do to get them to the finish line, in the process more effectively exercising their discipline muscle with less troublesome battle in the brain.

To me, a system is something that allows you to get to your result with less effort and by doing the things you should do but don't necessarily want to do. The effectiveness of the system, therefore, relies on how much friction is eliminated from all the things you "should" do. For example, if I had to wash and process all the ingredients for the green smoothie every day, I wouldn't do it.

Among other problems, the consequences of not working with a system are inefficiency and a greater reliance on luck resulting from ad hoc behaviors, where failures are hard to

---

aerobic strength at least two days a week. That this turned into widespread advice to "exercise three days a week" appears to be dumbed-down guidelines to make them "workable" for a less-than-ambitious public.

identify and correct. The choice is simply to hodgepodge our way around without systems and stay stuck in status quo, or get fat (or both), or use a system. After I read about this concept years ago, the fact that the successes in my life were due to adequately defined systems became obvious. Equally, the acknowledgment that the failures happened for the same reason felt like being slapped in the belly with a wet fish, as my dad would say.

Similar to other successes in your life, your legal matter may be systemized. Although implementing systems in other areas of life is often challenging and falls in the "I know that—but still don't do it" basket of ways we make life complicated, this How Not To Get Screwed By Your Lawyer system is easy.

It simply encourages you to take the steps necessary to:

- Stay organized with paperwork, communications, money matters, timelines, tasks, and progress.

- Communicate more effectively.

- Better use your skills to manage your lawyer, with the ultimate goal of saving money on your fees and bringing a measure of control back to your legal matter.

It's been popular to talk about systems in recent years following the advice from Scott Adams. But systems are not a fad. When the privileged began spending six dollars for four ounces of celery juice that costs twelve cents to produce and that my sixth-grade-educated mother was making over thirty years ago

ecuting on the System

how do we implement a system in this context? Start with a oject management tool.[12] Before you say, "I don't like any" or hat's too complicated for my legal issue," it's possible to use in-old regular file folders. However, I think it's better if you a digital platform like Airtable, Trello, Monday, Asana, or atever you are used to.

is tool will let you house all the steps and processes that go the system. In the next few chapters, I'll give you plenty xamples of how to build it out. Basically, you want a tool to your system take shape. You need a place to keep different uments organized properly. You need a room that reminds what your next step is, and you need a layout that keeps r timeline straight.

TIPS TO EXECUTE

are a few tips for creating a system and making a project agement tool work for you.

---

er project management tools like Airtable are geared toward data manage-
ut can still be highly effective (I like and use this tool for multiple project
ement purposes). Excel and its slightly less backward cousin, Google Sheets,
appropriate because they don't have the capacity to house all your relevant
documents in an easy and "one-place" format.

with a no-name juicer from the obscure health food store she found it in, celery juice became a fad.

Systems are not. The way they've been packaged and resold may be faddish, but they are an essential component to understanding habits and their success or failure.

By the end of this chapter, you'll understand how to start putting your How Not To Get Screwed By Your Lawyer system together and how to pick a tool that will help you best execute on this. In the following chapters, we'll work to systemize the lessons so that you can easily carry out the steps necessary to ensure you accomplish your goals when it comes to your lawyer.

YOUR SYSTEM, YOUR UNDERWEAR

Think of the system that you need to achieve your objectives as your underwear. First, no one else's belongs on you, and yours don't belong on anyone else. Second, the system—kind of like your underwear—holds everything in place. Anatomically or situationally, things are unwieldy when they're not on.

Now, it's up to you to define point B as the end of your legal matter. Take ownership of where you want this legal matter to take you so that you can define those terms and express them clearly to your lawyer. For example, in litigation, is your objective to reach a quick and reasonable settlement? Or is it to fight to the bitter end to establish a precedent that you and your business will not settle, so your opposition should not sue you unless they're prepared for a long fight?

Once that strategic direction is established, your system should reflect the steps and processes to get you from point A (where you're starting) to your defined point B. Having the end in mind will help you choose the appropriate steps to get you to your stated objective at point B, encourage your lawyer to stay focused on those stated objectives, and more effectively track your and your lawyer's progress as you approach those stated objectives.

Systems Created with Expertise

If you hire an employee or independent contractor, you probably have a system, maybe in the form of a standard operating procedure, to do that. You or someone from your team identifies the job requirement, drafts the job description, reaches out to your network in some established way or otherwise notifies the marketplace of the opportunity, reviews résumés based on established criteria, and otherwise finalizes a decision. To the extent you are following some sort of established process when doing so, you've established a system for the hiring process.

Just because you create your own system doesn't mean it's the best. Chances are you have benefited from experience and expertise in the human resources arena to hone the processes that became your system.

As you proceed to create your own system based on this chapter and the ones that follow, I encourage you to supplement it with the experience you've gained, if any, from your past dealings

with lawyers, as well as any other intelligence lated in developing systems in other areas of yo

For very strange reasons, we often have skills brilliantly in some contexts and supremely For example, I don't have much patience wit But when it comes to children and old peop haven't figured out the art of taking my pa applying them to all age groups. What's w about this shortcoming for at least twenty-f not fully fixed. I don't know why.

You may be more perfect than me and not ha problem. It's not my place to say. It is for me have you employed in your business life? In Have you used them to the same degree—o it comes to dealing with your lawyer? If yo there are any number of skills you've used things like grit, determination, and per those alone will help you with your lawyer being a bit of a victim such that it has pre tion of the skills already at your disposal? *your business?* I'm guessing not. So why c that we have in one place and use them ev

Touching on what we already covered in a system will help us make the best use c It will help us keep track of where we are importantly, it will help us overcome any s place. While we may have played the vi our lawyers, we can avoid that role by im

E

So
pr
"T
pla
us
wh

Th
int
of e
let
doc
you
you

Her
man

12 Ot
ment b
manag
are not
data an

It's Not about the Tool

Lance Armstrong, before being embroiled in controversy, wrote *It's Not about the Bike.*[13]

The tools rarely matter (whether you're on illegal high-performance drugs or not; he was far from alone). When I raced triathlons, I did a bunch of research on wetsuits and bikes. And even though it was nice to know for sure what I needed and what was going to give me an edge, it wasn't anything that helped me finish. That "edge" only mattered if I was headed for competitive racing. Age grouper? Not important. Of course, I was always trying to do my best and improve my times. But the equipment wasn't what made the difference. Some of you might have a cutting-edge gym in your home with a Peloton®. But you still might be out of shape. Maybe some others have a few loose dumbbells lying around with P90X® DVDs from 2005 and you're stronger than ever.

It's not the Peloton versus the old DVDs that makes the difference but the system in place for making the workouts happen. We won't belabor the point about the system being the key because there's another aspect of the system that involves heart. Like Rocky Balboa compared to the Russian dude. They both had systems. But they still needed heart, and heart defined the win.

---

13   Lance Armstrong, *It's Not about the Bike* (New York: Putnam, 2000).

Here's the rub: pick something that you will commit to using. Something that you'll have some heart about.

Use What You Know

If you're already familiar with a tool and you use it in other parts of your life, use that one, even if you don't love it.

For example, I like Trello but don't love it. But it's not worth getting sidetracked trying to learn something new when my team already uses it effectively. Besides, all tools have their limitations. In the following chapters, you'll see how simple the concepts will be to execute, so for now, just pick a tool.

Pick Something That Is Easy to Access on All Devices

Be sure to have the tool on your commonly used devices so that you have quick access to reflect information in real time. All the tools I've already mentioned are cloud-based applications with mobile-friendly features that easily allow you to do that.

If You Really Hate Digital, Go Paper

A workable system could absolutely and legitimately be a paper copy. Understand, however, that a "file" that you dump everything into is *not* a system. A group of files might be the portal through which you execute the system, but you'll still need to build out the processes that allow you to actually get stuff into your system.

Don't Make This Complicated

As much as I hate babysitting and haven't done it since I was a child, I will happily babysit you, if you wish. If you just don't care and want me to make the decision for you, then just use Trello. At the time of this printing, Trello gives me nothing and doesn't know me from Alexa. Like I said, I don't even love it. I like Airtable better, but for this purpose, Trello works a little better.

You're welcome.

As you can see, there are ways to take a systematic approach regardless of what type of system you use. There are more examples and illustrations in action at manageyourlawyer. com/tools if you need more help, or you can also scan the QR code below.

But honestly, just pick a tool and move on.

The good stuff is coming up.

SYSTEM SUGGESTIONS

Create a new project in your preferred project management tool, and create some basic categories such as:

- Before I Hire My Lawyer

- Preliminary Steps

- Month 1

- Ongoing

- Completed

We'll use these or similar headings to build out the steps based on the rest of the material in this book. Visit manageyourlawyer.com/systems for more tutorials on this process or scan the QR code below:

CHAPTER 3

COMMUNICATIONS FOR JOY OR TRAUMA

IF YOU'RE A PASSIONATE ITALIAN LIKE ME, YOU KNOW
what that translates into at the dinner table. It's fiery and
dramatic. People often sound angrier than they are, and calmer
people can't handle it. But what that often means is you're
passionate in the moment and couldn't care less moments
later. Which is why I could leave a stressful day of long work
and still have hot boyfriends.

Admittedly, the Mediterranean-blood form of communication
is not everyone's cup of tea, and you don't usually get what you
want without some honey, no matter how smart or right you
might be.[14] But even if honey isn't your style, there are lots of
ways to make different communication methods effective.

---

14 Admittedly, the Mediterranean-blood form helps those of us who are commu-
nication-challenged to be highly entertaining to have a drink or go on an adven-
ture with. In general, developing skills to overcome persistent shortcomings is
completely possible and desirable.

We all have skills and shortcomings. Lawyers do too. Some lawyers have more skills than shortcomings; others have more shortcomings than skills. Just because a lawyer communicates effectively with a subset of clients that appreciates their services doesn't mean they are a good communicator with their subordinates, their kids, or the barista that morning.

Similarly, you may struggle with your communication, depending on the person and situation.

This chapter will give you supersonic rules for better communication with your lawyer. These rules may help you in other contexts as well, but the suggestions below specifically have your lawyer in mind.

To make this exercise more fruitful, as you're working through the list, take an honest look at what you're doing or have done with your lawyer in the past, or if you don't have that specific experience to draw on, think about your communication style with other professionals. Have you been *too* quiet or *too* suspicious or not listened carefully enough because you were struck by how much your lawyer's face looked like a billable clock? Also, try to evaluate what you *do* compared to what you *know*. We all have knowledge. But just because we know we should eat more vegetables doesn't mean we do.[15] Take honest stock of your *actions*, not words or thoughts or shoulds.

---

15   "Men, Younger Adults, and People Living in Poverty Get Fewest Fruits/Vegetables," Centers for Disease Control and Prevention, November 16, 2017, https://www.cdc.gov/media/releases/2017/p1116-fruit-vegetable-consumption.html. The CDC says only one in ten people eat enough vegetables.

Allison Aubrey and Maria Godoy, "75 Percent of Americans Say They Eat Healthy—Despite Evidence to the Contrary," NPR, August 3, 2016, https://www.npr.org/sections/thesalt/2016/08/03/487640479/75-percent-of-americans-say-they-eat-healthy-despite-evidence-to-the-contrary. Also, 75 percent of adults say they eat healthy.

I'm practicing all of these myself. Let's practice together.

UNDERSTAND WHY WE SPEAK DIFFERENTLY AROUND DIFFERENT PEOPLE

SCENARIO

Ferdinand needs an intellectual property lawyer to discuss a product design. Other than the basic concept of intellectual property protection, he doesn't know much about the process.

He meets with an IP lawyer, Isabella.

Ferdinand acknowledges that he's a successful business-man. But subconsciously, he sees Isabella as the more powerful figure given her expertise and the education that is necessary to deal with his intellectual property problem. He uses a very professional tone and acts with a pretense that he generally understands the subject but needs guidance.

Isabella maintains her lawyerly air and explains the process using legalese that Ferdinand doesn't fully understand. Not wanting to sound stupid, he holds back his questions. Isabella surmises that she's not made herself clear, so she creates a timeline that explains the process more clearly.

It's a simple example of communication accommodation theo-ry,[16] an area of human behavior developed in 1971 by Howard Giles, a professor of communications at the University of California. Generally, the theory examines how people seek to gain approval and create a positive image by adjusting communication through words or gestures depending on situations and who they are communicating with.

Surely, we can all think of at least one example where we were either Ferdinand or Isabella. There's likely a Ferdinand *and* an Isabella in all of us. According to the theory, Ferdinand uses a process of convergence because he tries to adapt to Isabella's more complex language. Isabella first uses divergence in accentuating the social and nonverbal communication differences, but she also tries to bridge that gap later by reading Ferdinand's body language to recognize that she needs to adjust her language so that he can more easily understand the complex issues.

Taking this closer to home, do you speak to your golfing buddy the same way you speak to your spouse? To your mother? To your priest? Is that obnoxious comment you leave on social media what you'd say in person?

Instead of burying ourselves in the safety of theoretical details, let's think about how we can use the data and theory to our advantage.

As discussed in the Introduction, you may naturally take a deferential stance when you hire a lawyer simply by virtue of

---

16 Howard Giles and Tania Ogay, "Communication Accommodation Theory," *Explaining Communication: Contemporary Theories and Exemplars*, 2007, https:// core.ac.uk/download/pdf/147103741.pdf.

the inherent nature of the relationship. This is common even among successful business owners who have no problem standing up for themselves.[17] In fact, I know a scientist and businessman with multiple successful businesses and not a shy bone in his body who once remarked, "Even I sometimes get intimidated by my lawyer!"

To change that deferential attitude (which you're doing by reading this book), start by acknowledging this behavioral tendency of diverging with the person perceived as having the higher social status (your lawyer). That manifests in some predictable ways. For example, you may not ask the questions you want to ask or take on similar behaviors that protect your lawyer's perception of you (i.e., that you're not dumb).

Note that even if you generally think all lawyers are snakes, there's still the inherent reality of your business purpose for them, and in those moments, you need them, giving them the "higher social status."

An acknowledgment and understanding of your own behavior helps you go into the relationship with the right headspace. That heightened sense of awareness will allow you to recognize and get past your natural convergence or divergence tendencies.

---

17 "2019 Legal Trends Report," Clio, accessed May 19, 2022, https://www.clio.com/resources/legal-trends/2019-report/.

Clio's Legal Trends Report 2019 found that 40 percent of millennials "admit to being intimidated by lawyers compared to 30% of Gen X and only 20% of Boomers." I have no reason to doubt the study, although like all methodologies, it raises some questions. How many people, whether asked anonymously or not, would admit to being intimidated by a lawyer? Moreover, as discussed in the communication adaptation theory, a person may adjust their behavior as if they were intimidated, even if they did not necessarily feel intimidated; deference in essence lends itself to intimidation. My guess is these stats underreport the intimidation factor.

ESTABLISH COMMUNICATION PREFERENCES AT THE OUTSET OF YOUR RELATIONSHIP

Some things that sound trite aren't. Communication, or lack thereof, is often a catalyst for the breakdown of relationships between lawyer and client. At the beginning of the engagement, it's helpful to establish how information will be passed from one to the other. Does your lawyer want to be notified by phone or email? What's your preferred communication method, and if different from your lawyer's, how do you plan to balance the two?

Even if there's friction—for example, if you prefer the phone and your lawyer wants email[18]—compromising early on through a simple and short conversation will set expectations. Open lines of communication help ensure no one misses important information and details are properly memorialized. They tend to keep the mood happy too.

Engagement letters, which we'll cover in Chapter 6, are usually the best time to address communication preferences.

BEING QUIET, DISCIPLINED, AND A GOOD LISTENER DOES NOT A SUBMISSIVE DOG MAKE

My sweet mutts love to roll over on their backs for belly rubs. But even if you like to roll over and get a belly rub now and again, you needn't become submissive to do it.

---

18 Obviously, a preference for phone calls should not replace a paper trail for the purpose of organization or protection. You can write up a quick memo and put it in an appropriate place in your project management file. The quickest thing to do is to use a transcription service that lets you record some notes and have them immediately transcribed for download.

Listening carefully, making notes, and asking nicely for what you need is easy. Yet, we don't execute as much as we should.

- "Can you repeat that?"

- "Let me repeat that back to you to make sure I'm understanding correctly."

- "I'm sorry, but can you slow down a little? These concepts are new to me."

- "Let's back up if you don't mind."

These all go a long way to prevent lollygagging through a mud pit.

And don't worry if you don't have the "perfect conversation" the first time around. For some, getting through a conversation with even one question asked is a big start to better asserting what you need.[19] Continue to practice.

---

19 James Clear, *Atomic Habits* (New York: Penguin Random House, 2018).

This idea cannot be emphasized enough. Our failures are often the result of a desire and expectation that massive change is necessary to bring the results we seek. When I created my first online program in health and wellness, I had my clients itemize small incremental changes from week to week to beat the assured failure that comes with, "Starting January 1, I'm going to eat right, exercise, drink more water, lay off the sauce, and meditate every day!" Anyone who's had a regular gym membership has seen firsthand the difference in traffic on January 2 and January 31 and understands this perfectly. Clear covers the topic of "atomic"-sized habits contributing to "remarkable results" beautifully.

LAY IT ALL OUT CLEARLY
AND IN WRITING

There is a lot of emotion involved in legal matters that can cloud our recollection. Even business deals. We want the better side of negotiations. We want the deal. And we want to celebrate with a bottle of something.

Writing things down forces us to articulate thoughts fully. It's the sail to the ship or the wind to the sail. Organizing thoughts in written form ahead of a meeting, for example, could ensure all relevant details are passed on for a better understanding of the case at hand, make for a shorter meeting, and when you hand your lawyer a copy of your notes, avoid requiring a secretary to type them up later.

To make this writing exercise more effective, keep the following tips in mind:

Create a Process to Ensure You Write Things Down while They Are Fresh

Do this even if it feels agonizing to have to relive the unpleasant circumstances that led you to this particular time and place, putting you in front of your lawyer. For example, you can do as I do and record your notes while walking the dog. There are only two places I keep those thoughts: if written, in my "Notes" feature accessible on both my Mac and iPhone or if a recording, directly into my otter.ai account (you could simply choose your smartphone recording feature). But that's just the temporary depository that still needs to be organized. Every Friday morning, I take all those scattered ideas and put them in their appropriate folders and files. In this particular case, you would take those notes and apply them to a "To Discuss with My Lawyer" card or area of your project management system. If once a week is not often enough, you can make it every day or any clearly identifiable interval you designate.

If You're Trying to Impart Detailed Information like Dates, Times, or Circumstances, Write It All Down

Take time to do it fully and in chronological order. Your lawyer may find value in a fact that you don't think is important. Better for you to get organized in those details than to assign what would otherwise be an unproductive task to your lawyer, charging lawyer rates. This is part of your or your team's job. Making it your lawyer's is like paying a secretary lawyer's rates. It's inefficient.

If Writing Slows You Down, Use a Transcription Service

There is a wide selection to help you. Record your details and use a transcription service. Then, carefully review and edit the work.

As You're Writing, Use Proper Grammar as Best You Can

The clearer you are, the less time your lawyer will need to spend trying to decipher your meaning. Worse, being unclear puts you at risk for your lawyer missing something important.

Don't Assume Your Lawyer Has Read Something Just Because You Sent It to Them

Ask very specifically, "Did you read what I sent you?" If they say something like, "I took a quick look at that, but why don't we go over it again," they probably didn't read it. What you want to avoid is duplicating efforts. If the lawyer has read it, you don't need to reiterate the same information they have on paper at a meeting or over the phone. But equally, you want to make sure the lawyer is clear on the information. So you can ask things like, "Do you have any questions about what I've provided?" or "Do you need more information?"

If you'd like to go deeper into these writing tips, visit manageyourlawyer.com/communicate or scan the QR code below:

BE DETAILED BUT NOT IRRELEVANT

It's your lawyer's job to determine which facts are relevant. So err on the side of providing more information than less. At the same time and depending on your legal matter, your lawyer doesn't need to know the exact degree to which you hate the other guy in your breach of contract case.

BE HONEST

Outside the criminal law context where your lawyer may tell you they don't want to know, be honest. Really dig into this. Do you omit facts or information because you're embarrassed, you're afraid, you think it's unimportant, or you hate exposing your vulnerable side? How do you balance needing to give your lawyer personal information, knowing that you don't totally trust them?

Acknowledge that this may be an issue for you. If it isn't, move on. But if it is, start evaluating how your natural tendencies might lead you astray and prevent your lawyer from helping you as best they can.

BATCH UPDATES AND QUESTIONS

We'll talk about organization in the next chapter, but the concept of batching comes in handy here. As a general rule, there's inefficiency in stopping and starting a new task. When it comes to your lawyer, there's often a direct cost to that inherent inefficiency because of the hourly billing structure. You should communicate information in batches rather than sharing one piece of information here and another over there.

We'll get into examples of how this translates into higher bills in Chapter 10. Suffice it to say, for the moment, that there is less cost involved when you can batch your communications.

AS SOON AS AN ISSUE ARISES, DEAL WITH IT

Annoying things fester. And then they mutate, further infecting our hearts and souls and clouding our brains. You can ignore it for a time. Until you can't.

You know exactly what I'm talking about. Whether it's with your lazy business partner, an unreliable supplier, or a no-show employee (or a spouse, parent, or difficult child), it just stews into a big, smelly pile.

When a problem presents itself, raise it with your lawyer in a polite conversation, and correct course. Don't wait to "see if things get better." They're unlikely to.

USE YOUR LAWYER AS PRACTICE

I remember telling a friend that I didn't think it was going to work out with some guy I was dating. The advice she gave me was advice I've been able to use many times in everything from relationships to business, and I'm passing it on as good advice is best done.

She said to use him as practice. My immediate response was to think it was demeaning. Then I realized there was no disrespect to either me or the soon-to-be ex. The point was that unless I planned to break up with him tomorrow, in the meantime I should practice being a better person in the relationship and improve my communication with him.

Consider that practicing improvement in your communication style with your lawyer is an opportunity for practice in more important relationships in your life. As we just mentioned in Chapter 2, sometimes we're good at things with some people but not others.

Nonetheless, it's also the case that when we get better at something in one area of life, there's at least greater scope to get better in other areas.

Practice at least one new communication skill with your lawyer. Your lawyer is your advocate and will in all likelihood want to help you along, and they may want to improve themselves.

Just imagine who else in your life might benefit.

SAMPLE CONVERSATIONS

Let's look at a couple of scenarios.

The Old You

You: Our company has developed a new product, and I was hoping you could give me some information on the patent process.

Lawyer: Sure! It's unfortunately a highly administrative area of the law. Are you looking to file a provisional patent or a utility patent?

You (silent voice): How in God's name would I know?

You (outside voice): You'll need to explain the difference to me.

Lawyer: Sure. The provisional patent is a temporary patent that is less costly and requires less documentation. It's not reviewed by the patent office and offers incomplete protection, but it at least ensures the earliest possible date for a patent filing. The design patent is more complicated but offers more protection for your invention, although no protection is ironclad.

You (silent voice): What the fuck does that mean?

You (outside voice): I see.

Lawyer: So I'll need an additional retainer to file the motion.

You (silent voice): Just casually slither that in...

You (outside voice): Sure.

The New You

You: Our company has developed a new product, and I was hoping you could give me some information on the patent process.

Lawyer: Sure! It's unfortunately a very complicated and highly administrative area of the law. Are you looking to file a provisional patent or a utility patent?

You (reinvented voice): I have no experience with patents, and you'll need to explain the difference to me.

Lawyer: Sure. The provisional patent is a temporary patent that is less costly and requires less documentation. It's not reviewed by the patent office and offers incomplete protection, but it at least ensures the earliest possible date for a patent filing date...

You (reinvented voice, politely interrupting): I'm sorry. I don't understand the practical implications. Can you explain that in context of my specific question regarding my company's new patents?

Lawyer: Of course (gives you a better explanation that relates specifically to your matter).

You: Great! I understand, although I'd like to clarify the timeline.

Lawyer: (Explains the timeline) So I'll need an additional retainer to begin the patent process.

You: I already paid you the first retainer and haven't yet received an itemized account, so I'll need to see that first. Also, I think we're jumping the gun based on what you've told me. We'll have to get back in touch once we've settled on the final design.

Lawyers will often give you the general lay of the land, which the lawyer did in this case by explaining the difference between provisional and nonprovisional patents. While that is sometimes helpful, you need to understand how the law applies to your specific issue. Unless there is a good business reason for it and it assists with your understanding, paying for a law lesson is unnecessary.

SYSTEM SUGGESTIONS

On your Trello board under Ongoing, create a card called Communication Musts. Summarize the principles discussed here, and in particular the ones you know you need to work on. Plan a five-minute audit following each meeting or communication with your lawyer to record your notes on your communication wins and failures.

Visit manageyourlawyer.com/communicate or scan the QR code below for examples on what this might look like in practice.

CHAPTER 4

ORGANIZE FOR THE WIN

Business never ceases to amaze me, especially how the right spin can turn organizing messy sock drawers into a business conglomerate worth millions. It's what a soft-spoken organizational consultant from Japan did to create a cult following.

For that to happen, it had to be about more than organizing sock drawers. And maybe even more than just a good marketing strategy.

We'll get into that in this chapter, and by the end of it you'll know that:

1. Organizing is not hokey.

2. Organizing can save you boatloads of cash that is guaranteed to be more productively used in your pocket rather than your lawyer's.

3. Organizing may even help you strategize your legal matter better.

THE BIG PICTURE

Marie Kondo's *The Life-Changing Magic of Tidying Up*[20] is about organizing your brain as much as it is finally learning to keep chronically disorganized drawers tidy. It's about what happens after people tidy up and surround themselves with things that bring them joy. The consultant-turned-author found her clients went on to write books, start businesses, get better jobs, or discover better relationships—any number of fundamental changes people desire to make when the time is right but "right" never comes. Apparently, that freeing of the physical clutter frees the mind to help see the bigger picture and greater opportunities.

The Kondo method is about orchestrating a space to transform a life. That easily explains the five million copies sold of the first book, which led to more books, a Netflix special, $89 cardboard organization boxes (among a host of other beautifully curated products sold on her website), and perhaps most profitable of all, a $2,200 certification program with a $500-per-year membership fee to teach others how to teach others this life-changing organization stuff.

---

20 Marie Kondo, *The Life-Changing Magic of Tidying Up: The Japanese Art of Decluttering and Organizing* (Berkeley: Ten Speed Press, 2014).

Voilà! A worldwide phenomenon and multimillion-dollar enterprise was solidified into modern culture.

When you strategically clear a few of the trees, you free your mind to see the forest, which potentially leads to better strategy and execution of your path in and out of that forest.

Let's drop the awkward feeling about "organizing" and the cultness of anything referred to as "life-changing" and consider the strategic opportunity it represents.

First, better organization gives you greater opportunities to avoid duplicating efforts, allows you to better manage lawyers and staff involved in your representation, makes decision-making more efficient, leads to more comprehensive schedules and timelines, and generally improves productivity. Each of those benefits can easily translate into cost savings.

Second (and interestingly), better organization tends to lead to less stress and anxiety. That's not hard to appreciate. When you are engaged in a project with clearly articulated tasks, expectations, and schedules, there's less need for WD-40®. When time is wasted with gears grinding unpleasantly, frustration and anxiety tend to result.

Finally, although your lawyer is ultimately responsible for the strategic direction of your matter, you must *own* that direction and understand your choices, obligations, and responsibilities along the way. The extent to which that is laid out in an organized fashion will dictate how you contribute to the strategy of your legal case and how that strategy is played out. At a minimum, your understanding of your contribution can make a world of difference in setting expectations more appropriately.

So we need to organize several things:

TIME

Money comes and goes. Stuff comes and goes. People and relationships come and go. But time just goes. Whoever is responsible for expressing that truth, it works out very nicely for lawyers.

As good as lawyers are at billing their time, two can play that game. You can also be good at tracking some of your own time. In fact, you're going to channel Marie Kondo like she's never been channeled. If you are present at meetings, your time will be tracked. If you've spent an hour reviewing an agreement, track it.

We'll get to how to do this in a minute (it's a piece of cake), but you're likely asking why this is important at all since the only time that can be tracked is time you actually spend with your lawyer, and you certainly can't track what they are doing.

There are a few reasons.

1. Small Often Feels Big

Notice that small amounts of work can feel *big*. Legal stuff may feel like that because it's so emotionally draining. Even if your time is not being billed and paid like a lawyer's, you should have a crystal-clear idea of how much time it's sucking. What are the parts that need you, and what are the parts that can be outsourced? All those productivity books might be boring, but they have a point when they tell us to take stock of where our time is going.

But it needs to be *honest*. Not where you think your time is going but where it's actually going. About one in ten people eat the recommended dose of fruits and vegetables, but if you were to ask people if they eat enough fruits and vegetables, there's almost a 100 percent chance that more than one in ten people will say yes.

Vague and loose recollections, or your perceptions, are not always accurate. (Note also that an accurate idea of your time required in the matter will be necessary in the larger cost-benefit analysis as to whether to carry through with any particular legal matter.)

2. The Hoax of the Hourly Rate

You are fully aware, with every fiber of your being and nook and cranny of your soul, of the hourly billing arrangement you've agreed to with your lawyer. And yet...

...we kind of forget. It's why even if you're billed weekly, the bills are always a surprise. These ten minutes here and a couple of hours there slip into our nether regions, never to be found again. Whether that's because it's an unconscious maneuver to keep us sane, we're overly polite, or it's simply that the rest of life is too busy to worry about this unimportant-in-the-grand-scheme-of-things-but-utterly-wealth-defying circumstance is unclear.

Better tracking practices will remind you about the quickly passing time.

3. The Deposit Disorder

Something weird happens when a deposit is paid (or a retainer is paid to a lawyer, which we'll get into in Chapter 7). It feels like a sunk cost. Now, it could become a sunk cost, but it's not at all necessarily a sunk cost. You can't assume a sunk cost until something happens to make it a sunk cost (while avoiding the sunk cost fallacy—the idea that in the process of continuing a behavior, one considers past investment that prevents the best course of action).

This is somewhat of the opposite problem. Money is paid, and because it's already paid, it's somehow devalued, treated prematurely as a sunk cost.

That is not at all how we should be viewing a retainer, and tracking payments helps us keep track of investments on which we are owed a return.

We'll get into this more in Chapter 7.

4. Easier Reconciliation

We'll discuss bill reconciliation in a couple of chapters, but if you don't have details, there won't be much reconciliation to do. You will guess. Imagine your accountant sitting in front of you as you come up with numbers from your recollection.

DOCUMENTS

Things get unruly quickly. Like after you pull out your shirt and pants and decide you don't want to bother unpacking the rest of your suitcase for a two-day business trip. Besides, there's hardly anything in there. You'll be really careful to pull things out and keep it neat. By dinnertime, it's a mess. Such is the case with your file marked "Legal."

IN REAL LIFE

Petunia was ready to make an exit and sell her business, Small Technology Co., to Huge Technology Co. for a decent profit. In the course of due diligence, Huge Technology Co. discovered that Petunia's books were a disaster. Improper or missing records pertaining to shareholder disputes, several significant corporate actions like acquisitions and dispositions of businesses and intellectual property, and regular business left the books in disarray. Huge Technology Co. refused to close (and could not legally close) until the books were put in order. It took a highly skilled and experienced paralegal several weeks, ultimately comprising fully one-third of the total legal bill, to render the books in suitable condition for the deal to close. Petunia was furious, but her desire to get this deal done made the work necessary.

The Moral

Anyone can hand a big mess to a lawyer, but understand you'll pay for someone else to organize it, and it's easy to lose something valuable in thick weeds.

Ensure a suitable person is organizing your documents. In most cases, that's someone on your team who knows the business and knows the company. Things can be fixed if need be, but if a law firm is doing it, it's bound to be more costly than it otherwise could be done.[21]

Your project management system should have several places for important documents. Basically, you'll want to have a section for documents and subsections for certain types of documents. This takes mere minutes to set up, and then you just have to decide how often you will ensure everything gets into the right section. That timing will depend on the time-sensitive nature of your matter.

---

21 A colleague of a colleague worked with a lawyer who billed his secretaries at $140 per hour as "e-commerce specialists." Even if a law firm is organizing documents on your behalf, ensure you are billed appropriately.

Visit manageyourlawywer.com/tools or scan the QR code below if you'd like to see examples of this in practice.

COMMUNICATIONS

Everyone forgets things. Even important things. Keeping communications organized is equally important, for many of the same reasons we keep time and documents organized. As you set up your system for organizing documents, you can do the same for communications.

YOURSELF IN THE CONTEXT OF
YOUR LEGAL MATTER

As we just mentioned above, it's not just about the money. You can organize yourself better to contribute to a better overall strategy. Here are a few quick ideas.

Be Nice

In general, making things harder on your lawyer because you don't like him, the legal process, or an employee that morning doesn't do you any good. It may feel good on a Friday night to send a list of things you need by Monday morning, but it's a dumb thing to do, even if you're an investment banker who may still love doing it to young corporate attorneys.

The One Thing

Have a point to every conversation and meeting. What's the one objective going in, and what's the takeaway that designates tasks and purpose coming out?

Be Proactive with Your Attitude

What does it mean to be proactive? The *Cambridge Dictionary* defines it as "taking action by causing change and not only reacting to change when it happens."[22]

Yes, precisely.

You shouldn't wait for your lawyer to tell you what you need to do or what they're waiting for, nor should you always let them set the agenda. If your lawyer is waiting for some information, make sure they get it in a timely fashion. Don't give them another reason to say, "Well, I was waiting for you."

And if you find yourself wondering why you should go out

---

22   The *Cambridge Dictionary*, definition of proactive, https://dictionary. cambridge.org/dictionary/english/proactive.

of your way to get them the information they've requested quickly when you know you'll have to wait longer than you'd like, do it anyway. You go to the doctor on time knowing you're going to have to wait because you at least have a chance of getting in on time.

You're paying the lawyer. Make sure you're not the bottleneck preventing the provider from doing their job.

Be Proactive with Your Meeting Agendas

You don't have to wait for your lawyer to send you an agenda for a meeting. What do you want to ask? What do you need to bring up? Do you have new information that you need to share, and would this be the right time to do it? Are there new documents you need to address? Does this meeting need to be in person, or can a quick video or phone call handle it?

Be Proactive with Your Communication Style

Are you getting better at asking the questions you need to ask? Or are you still finding friction because you think you know but then you find you don't know as well as you would like? Do you leave messages for your lawyer and then say, "Well, I still haven't heard from him?" Or do you call too often? If it's clear you're not on the same page, tell your lawyer you don't want to be a pest, but you do want to ensure you get a call back in a reasonable time.

Be Proactive with Your Responses

Just because your lawyer said it, is it gospel? Does it require some additional thought or another expert? Does more discussion become necessary or important here? Do you need to temper that advice with other relevant advice? The pattern of "my lawyer said X; therefore, I must do Y" doesn't always have to stick. Your business judgment requires weighing the pros and cons taken in their entirety.

Better organizing yourself with these behaviors will help you optimize the relationship and allow you to contribute to the legal effort most effectively.

Organization Is Not Just about Marie Kondo-ing Everything

Have a sense of humor. As you create your system, title things in a fun way. If nothing else, you will be reminded that you're still the team owner. Instead of labeling a file "Project Disposition," consider:

- "Project Disposition: A New Chapter on Freedom"

- "Project Disposition: Going...Going...Gone"

- "Project Disposition: Dead Weight Ejected"

I would highly recommend something positive—despite the suggestions above—because the good life gurus tell us we should change our thoughts to change our life. I'm down with it. And you should be, too. Make it fun. Make it fresh. Make it a new start.

In fact, you can take this a step further by imagining yourself as your favorite strong character. Each of us has some character or real-life person we feel drawn to, who we admire, and who inspires us. It's good to admit that. Whether it's Superman, Elon Musk, or your favorite mentor or leader, there's a useful principle in imagining yourself as the kick-ass version of yourself that adopts the qualities you respect in another. Whichever character you choose, absorb the qualities that make that person great in your eyes, and approach this labeling—indeed, this entire project, including any and all dealings with your attorney—as that person.

SYSTEM SUGGESTIONS

To organize:

Time

Create a Meetings folder in the Month 1 section of your project. Create a single-page document called Meeting Log with three columns labeled Date, Duration, and Who Attended. **Also create a Time Spent on Legal Matter folder** in the Month 1 section of your project with a similarly created single-page document with appropriate headings (perhaps Date, Time Spent, and Activity). Then link these documents to the appropriate folders in your project management system.

(Don't be tempted to add notes in a Day-Timer® or calendar because then you'll end up with little bits of time scattered all over the place.)

Documents

Create a folder for Documents in the Month 1 section of your project. Depending on the size of your transaction, you may also need subfolders. (For example, for a large transaction, you may want to subdivide further into weeks or otherwise select a more suitable time interval.)

Communications

Create a folder for Communications in the Month 1 section of your project. Create subfolders depending on the types of documents relevant to your transaction (some examples will be provided in the following chapters).

Plan the remainder of the steps you will implement to make sure meetings, documents, and communications are properly organized. For example, as your meeting ends, immediately open up your meeting log and record pertinent details. You may choose to upload documents or forward them to a staff member immediately upon receipt—or you might schedule that in your calendar weekly on Friday mornings at 10:00 a.m. to make sure all these administrative tasks are completed.

CHAPTER 5

THE HIGH STAKES OF BORING PAPERWORK

WILD GUESS: THE LAST TIME YOU GOT A GYM MEMBERSHIP, installed new software, started your new phone contract, or took your kid whitewater rafting, you spent approximately four seconds, collectively, reading those voluminous electronic contracts they made you sign.

In a perfect world, it seems prudent to follow the advice of most lawyers and consumer advocates to read those types of agreements. In our less-than-perfect world, it's CYA advice with zero practicality. Although you might have some ability to make changes that reflect a more consumer-friendly tenor, what for? You're not likely to ask the overpriced dude ranch teaching you how to be a cowboy to cross out the part in the waiver that prevents you from suing if you get thrown off a horse or if one of their dozens of employees is negligent. The dudes will tell you to try crochet and send you on your honky-tonk way.

By all means, if you can get away with crossing out the part in the rafting company's waiver that says water activities can lead to paralysis or death, go for it. Otherwise, we don't practically have a choice to enjoy any number of adventurous or even what spoiled westernized world members of society like us would consider routine excursions in life. And with good reason since most businesses could not survive without such protections. So we cringe, sign, and hope nothing bad happens.

Your "standard" agreements with your lawyer, however—like engagement, fee, or retainer agreements—should be read carefully rather than glanced at casually. The difference between the waiver Tony Robbins makes you sign before walking barefoot over hot coals on the one hand and the engagement letter your lawyer asks you to sign on the other is that you can hardly do anything about the former, *whereas you absolutely can do something about the latter*. That's how I determine how much time I'm willing to invest in reading that boring-ass paperwork. As a practical matter, can I do something about this? If yes, I'll read. If no, I'll skim—at most. I'm not saying you should do what I do.

This chapter is about exploring three basic principles that recognize your unique capacity to do something about those agreements with your lawyer. They are also principles that every thinking and breathing human being can follow.

That's what we'll explore here, with the goal of discovering the tiger within you that is every bit as sharp as Beth Dutton in *Yellowstone* driving a knife into her latest target.

READ CAREFULLY

You'll never negotiate successfully if you have an "I'm stuck with it" attitude as an excuse to gloss over the words and sign. It's simply not consistent with a team owner approach. You won't even ask questions as productively as you could with that defeatist mentality. You won't apply any of the principles in this book as productively as you might otherwise.

The team owner approach starts with *carefully* reading all documents your lawyer expects you to sign. Because even if you have no Beth Dutton bone in your body—which would not be a bad thing, although at least a couple could be helpful—there is significant value in a commanding approach that at least acknowledges that you insist on understanding what your lawyer puts in front of you.

For some, this Beth-style approach will make a difference in how they feel, and therefore how they present themselves, in the lawyer-client relationship.

NEGOTIATION: THE FINEST OF ARTS

Negotiation skills are like golf. Or yoga. They can always be improved. Plus, working on them could help keep our brains sharp in the face of an increasing Alzheimer's risk.

You have negotiation and persuasion skills of some kind. If you are already a master at negotiation, great! Hopefully, you are already putting those skills to good use with your lawyer. If not, this book is your encouragement to do so. But no matter how strong or weak, every thinking human being has the capacity to improve these skills.

I am far from the best person to offer advice on negotiation or persuasion. What you'll find below is a simple summary of some basic principles that will put you in a better position to negotiate with your lawyer. The business client often forgets how much negotiating power they have, and money does indeed walk and talk. And you've got the wallet.

In following chapters, I'll also specifically point out negotiating opportunities as they become relevant. You don't need to be a "good" negotiator to make some progress with a prospective lawyer. Adopting just one of the principles here might be enough to set you on a stronger path.

You'll also find assembled at manageyourlawyer.com/negotiate some of my favorite resources on the topics of negotiation and persuasion (or scan the QR code below).

GIVE YOUR LAWYER A REASON TO NEGOTIATE WITH YOU: BECOME AN INCREDIBLE CLIENT

Show yourself to be a desirable client who even a busy lawyer wants. True, the better the lawyer, the less they will likely need your work. But all lawyers want and need work. It's part of their DNA. The good ones can be choosier for the right deal, the right time, and the right client.

So how do you become the right client? You can probably guess, but below you'll find simple ideas that put you in a better position to negotiate more effectively. I like to call this your client desirability quotient (CDQ). The more you improve in each of these areas, the higher your CDQ. Rank each of the following five factors out of ten, and then multiply by two and try to get to 100.

Be Respectful and Don't Be a Douchebag

Granted, d-bags are in the eye of the beholder. Still, lawyers are not all soulless robots. Do you, in the course of your business and business dealings, want to work with people with the personality of a snail? Or do you want to engage with dynamic, interesting people who you feel are serving their clients, their community, their state, their country, and the world? Lawyers want to enjoy the work they do for you, too.

Of course, there's no need to be naive about it, and we should stay fully aware that lots of people will take a dollar from anyone willing to pay it. Equally, there are many others who are very deliberate about the type of people they want to work for and with, recognizing that the long-term gains from that type of relationship will far outweigh the costs of hanging on to an asshole who happens to be a particularly good salesperson.[23]

Follow Instructions

Follow the rest of the chapters in this book. Seriously, I submit that as you better manage your lawyer with the techniques and processes in this book, you will consequently become a better client. Most lawyers are good people, and despite the profession's shortcomings, the best lawyers will want to work with good clients who are very much colleagues. If you approach your matter as the team owner, you act like a colleague and not a subordinate. And the most professional lawyers want that.

There's little or no downside to making things mutually beneficial. Just like it's always beneficial to incentivize both parties to an agreement to fulfill their obligations, it's more than okay to want to incentivize your lawyer to want to work with you for more than just the paycheck. That's where the magic happens.

----

23   Robert I. Sutton, *The No Asshole Rule: Building a Civilized Workplace and Surviving One That Isn't* (New York: Business Plus, 2007).

Despite appearances that it's the douchiest of lawyers profiting from their assholeness, there is ample evidence that although a company may benefit from assholes who bring in money short term, the long-term costs of keeping an asshole outweigh the gains they bring in.

Bundle Up

There are economic reasons your insurance company offers you a discount for buying more than one type of insurance. If there is scope for you to bundle up your legal needs, you can leverage potential cost savings the same way. Using different lawyers through the same law firm can yield similar benefits.

Consider further whether you have upcoming legal needs that, even if you're not ready to move forward with today, you can subtly and politely dangle like a carrot in front of a rabid rabbit.

IN REAL LIFE

Cornelius is a real estate developer with several deals a year. For his next deal, he requested a preferential billing rate from his long-standing attorney. Cornelius's lawyer successfully used the "Well, every deal is different" angle until Cornelius put his foot down. Because Cornelius had proven himself a valuable client with interesting and successful deals, all similar enough to justify some consideration, his lawyer was willing to do as he requested.

The Moral

Take a cue from GEICO®—it's possible fifteen minutes (of brainstorming on how you might bundle up your legal services) could save you 15 percent or more!

Bigger Is Usually Better

The bigger or more complex the legal matter, the higher the fees. And the higher the fees, the more a lawyer will want you as a client. The more a lawyer wants you as a client, the more scope there is to negotiate.

This is not to suggest that you should or could make a legal problem more challenging. Only that you should be aware of the complexity of your situation, to the best of your ability, in order to properly evaluate your negotiating position.

For example, let's say you need a straightforward employment agreement. It's unlikely that you will be able to negotiate fees that in this case may be set on a flat-fee basis. On the other hand, if you are entering a joint venture transaction with multiple partners in multiple jurisdictions involving complicated economics, that is something a qualified firm will salivate over.

Know Thyself

Finally, at the risk of sounding like a self-help Kool-Aid® slurper, just show the best side that is uniquely you. Not fake—just you. Everyone is different, and everyone wants to work with people they like. Let people see the best of you so they know if you will be a good fit. Presenting yourself as someone you are not is unlikely to yield a good result.

THE RISKS OF NEGOTIATING

You don't want to be obnoxious about negotiating, but does it hurt to ask?

Possibly.

Face it. Asking a bunch of questions or making demands can absolutely identify you as a "problem client."[24]

As a businessperson, you have to weigh that risk against your obligation to the financial health of your business. A prudent businessperson should be negotiating, lives to negotiate, has a responsibility to negotiate. This isn't about creating a fight or some drama and may not even need to enter the realm of negotiation. It may be enough to simply ask a few more questions and approach your lawyer in the manner outlined in this book.

Like in all cases of potential negotiation, it's also largely in the approach. There's no need to show up with a three-page list of questions or demands. And your intent is not to be difficult. You're asking because, as a prudent businessperson, your job is to understand your rights and obligations. Doing what you can to make wise business decisions, including through the course of your legal matter, keeps legal fees from getting out of control.

If a lawyer faults you for asking polite and intelligent questions, you may need to consider whether that's the right lawyer for you. There is almost always another good lawyer next door.

---

24 Similarly, jumping right into "How much do you charge?" may equally stereotype you as a bargain commodity shopper rather than a more sophisticated purchaser of professional services.

And when getting a new lawyer is not the right answer, then you've asked and accepted a no. That's still an improvement over the largely submissive status quo.

Chapter by chapter, that status quo is changing. And as we're heading into Chapter 6, we're about to hit that change big time.

SYSTEM SUGGESTIONS

If you'd like to pursue your education in persuasion and negotiation or perhaps even use your experience with your lawyer as practice to do so, consider incorporating time to read or learn. For example, since Fridays don't tend to be my most productive workdays, I like to use Friday afternoons for reading time. Perhaps during the course of your legal matter, your Friday afternoon can be dedicated to reading some of the works on persuasion and negotiation and using the upcoming week to practice at least one of the skills you read about, until the following Friday when you read and learn more and use that week for more practice, and so on.

Something like this has the fortunate consequence of producing at least one silver lining no matter how bad your legal matter turns out. (Knock on wood that won't be the case...I'm definitely rooting for you.)

CHAPTER 6

ENGAGEMENT LETTERS: MONTY PYTHON MEET LADY JUSTICE

OVER THE YEARS, I'VE HEARD PEOPLE COMMENT THAT they don't like movies because real life is so much more interesting. In the past, I always thought these people were missing out on the magic world of make-believe.

I'm now with those people and appreciate that real life is one giant Monty Python movie. Really, what in the fake world of movies can't be made more unbelievable by the real world?

The engagement letter your lawyer sends you to begin your enriching experience is a good example. Which is why we need to dedicate an entire chapter to them.

THE PRENUP OF THE LEGAL WORLD

The entire legal relationship starts with a lawyer (the person who presumably is in the greater negotiating position) sending the prospective client (the person in the lesser negotiating position) a legally dense agreement to establish the terms of the relationship between lawyer and client.

The agreements are often complex or hairy enough that lawyers may *recommend that prospective clients have another lawyer review them before signing.* Still, other lawyers hesitate to use them at all for the very reason that they will scare off prospective clients. And yet others believe that any hesitation by a client to sign an engagement letter could signify a problem child, so they use the engagement letter to weed those types out.

It's a bizarre circumstance for the honor of legal representation.

Despite the engagement letter setting out a client's rights and obligations, most people will tell you they rarely read them. At most, they skim them—mostly to find the space where they need to sign.

Not only do you need to understand your rights and obligations, but you should also appreciate where they work for you and where they don't, as well as where they present negotiating opportunities.

That's what this chapter is about. And it's a fun one. And even better news is that properly reviewing your engagement letter is a thirty-to-sixty-minute exercise. Piece of red velvet cake.

ATTITUDE

We covered this in the prior chapter, but it bears repeating since it is the most important thing that will make reading agreements with your lawyer more pleasant: the right attitude. Blindly accepting a document from your lawyer that you "have to" sign for the privilege of being accepted into a roster of clients is incongruent with your role as the team owner. It does not strengthen your negotiating position or make it easier to have a happy and productive legal experience.

> "Everything can be taken from a man but one thing: the last of the human freedoms—to choose one's attitude in any given set of circumstances, to choose one's own way."

Remember Viktor E. Frankl's words[25] as you set aside appropriate time to read your engagement letter, with a writing utensil to make appropriate notes. Grade school stuff. I told you this would be easy!

PUT THE PROVISIONS
IN YOUR OWN WORDS

You know how lawyers tend to write: annoyingly. Put the provisions of the engagement letter in your own words so you are crystal clear on what it is saying. Below is a sampling of how I might reword typical mincemeat provisions.

---

25 Viktor E. Frankl, *Man's Search for Meaning* (Boston: Beacon Press, 1962).

Example: The outcome of legal matters is uncertain and subject to many risks and variables. Prior results cannot and do not guarantee future results. Therefore, we have not made and cannot make any guarantees or promises regarding the outcome of this matter.

In other words: The justice system is so perverse, chaotic, and unjust that it's impossible to predict which way your case will go. You'll need to bear the brunt of that inherent reality, despite lawyers and judges having largely contributed to that perversity, chaos, and injustice. Sucks to be you.

Example: We have not and cannot predict your final fee.

In other words: The estimate we gave you is a crapshoot.

Example: Your fee will be calculated on the basis of our hourly rates, with allowances for reductions or increases in fees under certain circumstances.

In other words: Despite our firm holding you to payment terms, we can change them depending on the circumstances, which we won't define in advance.

Or you may find some letters actually defining some of those "circumstances" like this:

Example: You may have an emergency or urgent matter that requires us to cancel appointments, otherwise reschedule business, or impose other special demands on us; or your matter may require us to work outside normal business hours; or your matter may benefit from exceptionally successful representation. You understand and agree that any urgent request is subject to a minimum

$500 charge and that billing rates in these instances are double those set out in the fee schedule.

Read and understood [blank space for your initials ___].

In other words: Notwithstanding the fact that lawyers' hourly fees include the long hours we tend to work, if you call at an inopportune time, even during business hours, instead of using my judgment as to how to prioritize my files, I will double the rate I charge you if I turn my attention to your file—the one I already agreed to work on and even took a retainer for. And even though I'll find your signature at the end of this agreement, this particular clause has you bending over so far it requires an extra set of your initials.

Example: Your communications about us working for you are not engagements until that work is paid for via a retainer or as otherwise agreed.

In other words: If you haven't paid up front, your instructions to us will be ignored—despite what the Rules of Professional Conduct or any dumb court might say about our fiduciary obligations as your attorney.

Oh, and at the end of the letter, you are likely to find something to the effect of "Thank you for giving me and my firm the opportunity to serve you. I look forward to a long and mutually rewarding relationship."

After all that CYA fodder, how could the relationship be anything other than long and mutually rewarding?

Lawyers are artists. Poets. Confusion supremacists. My wild and very conservative guess with absolutely no basis is that among even the clients who read their engagement letters, most of them don't understand at least 50 percent of what is in them or the magnitude of how the provisions could affect them.

If ever there was a case for saying GFY to the legal industry, this might be it. Even though engagement letters bring benefits to both lawyers and clients, their nature makes them an ass-backward way to start a relationship.

This is all made worse by the fact that you can't practically say GFY because:

- That's a little rude, even for me.

- Maybe the lawyer you want is the best in class and you really want their representation.

- Bar associations everywhere require or at least recommend the use of engagement letters and even nonengagement letters—in the interest of promoting a transparent and reputable legal profession, naturally.

- As problematic as engagement letters are, problems would very likely be worse without them (another ringing endorsement of the legal system).

Now that we understand how batshit the world can be, let's attempt to make it better by diving into the common terms of an engagement letter with a little more gusto.

THE NUTS AND BOLTS
OF AN ENGAGEMENT LETTER

In the section above, you saw some examples of provisions you will find in engagement letters.

Those terms typically relate to:

- A clear enunciation of the party represented (e.g., is the client an individual or a business, partnership, or trust related to that individual?).

- What the lawyer is being hired for and what happens if that scope changes.

- The fee basis, including retainer requirements.

- Disclosure of conflicts and what happens in the face of conflicts.

- A few other odds and ends.

All of these items seem straightforward, but there are so many different legal relationships and complexities that cause even these "easy" details to be less clear. Let's explore those so you know what to watch for.

The Party Represented

Even defining who the lawyer acts for could be complicated. Does the lawyer act for the business or the individual? The partner or the partnership? The wife or the husband? The trust or the beneficiary?

Based on this alone, you can guess why this precision matters. And while you should expect that your lawyer is responsible for enunciating that, you should equally have a flavor for why it matters to help catch any oversight.

Fee Basis

Surprises can be fun but rarely when it comes to bills. The lawyer's billing practices should be clearly spelled out in the engagement letter. We will hit billing practices hard in the next couple of chapters, including areas you may wish to negotiate with respect to those billing practices. For now, let's deal with "ancillary fee issues," which you've already been introduced to in the sample provisions above and which will become even clearer in the following mock conversation:

You: Say, I noticed the engagement letter says you have the right to charge more in appropriate cases, and then you give me a bunch of examples of what those cases might be. I have some concerns with this.

Lawyer: It's our standard language.

You: Well, standard or not, you can understand why I might be concerned. What does "outside normal business hours" mean?

Lawyer: Our regular office hours are nine thirty to five Monday to Friday, excluding holidays, of course.

You: Of course. So if someone is working on my matter after five, you charge a higher rate?

Lawyer: Yes.

You: How much higher?

Lawyer: Twenty percent.

You: Huh. I take it working on weekends or holidays also entitles you to an additional 20 percent?

Lawyer: Yes, of course.

You: Interesting. Okay, well, maybe you can help me understand how you determine "exceptionally successful representation."

Lawyer: That generally refers to a scenario where you end up with a particularly good result—for example, if you end up with a really big settlement.

You: Aren't you *supposed* to get me a good result?

Lawyer: Of course.

You: Well, if you are bound by legal ethics to defend my interests to the best of your ability so that I end up with the best result possible, why is that considered "exceptionally successful"?

Lawyer: Sometimes a judge or jury will make an award that is beyond reasonable expectations.

You: So it's kind of like if my waiter provides excellent service and I leave a 30 percent tip?

Lawyer: You can think about it that way.

You: So on top of you, as a lawyer, not customarily being left a tip, you also get to decide how much the tip is?

Lawyer: [pausing] Well, not exactly.

You: So you'll come to me to ask how much of a tip I'd be willing to pay?

Lawyer: No, but we would make a reasonable assessment and apply it to your bill.

You: Uh-huh. What does that mean?

Lawyer: It would be based on the various circumstances.

You: I'm still not understanding why I can't decide if I'm willing to pay a tip or not and how much.

Lawyer: [Blank stare as his brain calculates whether you are too complicated a client to do his God's work for.]

You: And what do you classify as "special demands on us"?

Lawyer: That's where we might have to drop everything to address a court proceeding or otherwise try to take care of your special needs.

You: I see. But haven't you told me you're always going to address my needs?

Lawyer: Yes, but sometimes special needs are truly out of the ordinary.

You: Isn't that the nature of legal practice?

Lawyer: Yes, but it's not the nature of legal practice to have to drop everything else to take care of your matter.

You: Can you give me an example of when this might happen?

Lawyer: [sigh] Let's say the defendant files an emergency motion that we have to attend to in court. We're busy on other client work, but given time restrictions, we have to leave that other client work and deal with a response to your motion. That would be an example of where you might be required to pay a premium.

You: Are motions rare?

Lawyer: No, of course not.

You: Am I also required to pay a retainer?

Lawyer: Absolutely.

You: But that motion example could still be considered a special demand?

Lawyer: Yes, depending on the time at which it shows up.

You: I see. I guess I always thought part of lawyering was being prepared for anything.

Lawyer: What do you think about the agreement?

You: I think I'm getting screwed.

Fee disputes come up a lot (in addition to what would be a conservative guess that there are equally as many disgruntled clients who just pay their bill and walk away without expressing the feels, other than over a Skrewball peanut butter whiskey with a pal).

I can't say that these problems will go away just by knowing what is in your engagement letter. But you should know what to expect, and that includes knowing precisely how you will be billed and who will be working on your matter, to the extent possible.

Here's a good summary of billing issues to watch for in your engagement letter:

- Fee basis and rates: Ensure any oral arrangements are consistent with what is written in the engagement letter.

- Changes to fees: Lawyers often tell you this will happen without notice, but you should require notice.

- Allowances for premiums as described previously.

- Allowances for higher rates in defined or undefined circumstances, also as described previously.

Once you identify these matters, you can decide whether you want to raise the issue before signing the engagement letter or hope for the best. We'll discuss the pros and cons of each approach a little later.

Conflicts

A colleague seeking a divorce in a medium-sized city made sure he interviewed four of the best divorce attorneys in town. He hired one, and his soon-to-be-ex-wife attempted to hire each of the three others. As they had already consulted with her soon-to-be-ex-husband, they declined to take her matter.

Perhaps it wasn't right, but he had a drink and a laugh when he found out about her attempts.

Such is the issue of conflicts. You're likely familiar with the concept that lawyers must ensure there are no "conflicts of interest"[26] before they agree to work with you. Among larger firms in particular, the avoidance of conflicts is big business. It's even more sensitive for larger firms operating in multiple jurisdictions.

---

26 The ABA's Model Rules of Professional Conduct, Rule 1.7 addresses conflicts of interest. Paragraph 1 reads in part: "Loyalty and independent judgment are essential elements in the lawyer's relationship to a client. Concurrent conflicts of interest can arise from the lawyer's responsibilities to another client, a former client or a third person or from the lawyer's own interests."

Some jurisdictions have not adopted the model rules but have adopted them in part or in similar form.

Because of that, law firms will do what they can to get out of potential conflict issues. Even though there may be some ways of getting around conflict restrictions, law firms will try to escape the delicacy of having to obtain consent from their clients using an "advance conflict waiver" in the engagement letter. That provision essentially says that the client will agree, despite the law firm acting for that client, that the firm can represent a party adverse in interest to the client, without getting the client's approval.

You might be thinking, *Wait, the lawyer is asking me to consent to waive a conflict of interest before I know the circumstances or before I know it could be a problem for me and my business?*

You're correct. You are also right to wonder how a provision like this could be enforceable. Unfortunately, the ABA's commentary on the enforceability of this type of waiver, which I'd refer to as a "dark waiver," leaves clients in the dark.[27]

---

27 "Rule 1.7 Conflict of Interest: Current Clients-Comment," American Bar Association, accessed May 19, 2022, https://www.americanbar.org/groups/ professional_responsibility/publications/model_rules_of_professional_conduct/ rule_1_7_conflict_of_interest_current_clients/comment_on_rule_1_7/.

Comment 22 of Rule 1.7 of the Model Rules of Professional Conduct reads in full: [22] "Whether a lawyer may properly request a client to waive conflicts that might arise in the future is subject to the test of paragraph (b). The effectiveness of such waivers is generally determined by the extent to which the client reasonably understands the material risks that the waiver entails. The more comprehensive the explanation of the types of future representations that might arise and the actual and reasonably foreseeable adverse consequences of those representations, the greater the likelihood that the client will have the requisite understanding. Thus, if the client agrees to consent to a particular type of conflict with which the client is already familiar, then the consent ordinarily will be effective with regard to that type of conflict. If the consent is general and open-ended, then the consent ordinarily will be ineffective, because it is not reasonably likely that the client will have understood the material risks involved. On the other hand, if the client is an

Your jurisdiction, advice given by your state regulatory body, the interpretation of the ABA's guidance, case law, and the specific facts and circumstances of your unique scenario all play parts in determining whether this provision is enforceable against you. Furthermore, your understanding of the risk, your sophistication, your prior experience, and whether you were provided legal advice on the matter also play into whether this particular provision is enforceable.

This last paragraph is as unsatisfying as a James Bond movie without a Bond girl. A new car without the new car smell. Dinner without dessert. Yet, that's all I can offer. It's an uncertain area that is decided by different courts, different regulatory bodies, and different jurisdictions.

Given all that, and especially the part about your sophistication factoring into whether a law firm can use the advance consent provision against you, does that mean you should just play dumb if you find it in your engagement letter?

I can't offer that specific advice, but I can offer two guiding principles.

One, I'm generally not in favor of playing dumb when it comes to professional relationships—or *any* relationship. It just depends. Every human being is entitled to determine the

---

experienced user of the legal services involved and is reasonably informed regarding the risk that a conflict may arise, such consent is more likely to be effective, particularly if, e.g., the client is independently represented by other counsel in giving consent and the consent is limited to future conflicts unrelated to the subject of the representation. In any case, advance consent cannot be effective if the circumstances that materialize in the future are such as would make the conflict nonconsentable under paragraph (b)."

values by which they choose to live their life. There may be consequences you can live with, or there may not.

Two, given the highly uncertain landscape regarding advance conflict waivers, I'd be wary about agreeing to any such provision and would tell my lawyer that. They should acknowledge that uncertain landscape. There is nothing preventing them from asking for your consent down the road. You can tell them you will be happy to entertain a fair request for that accommodation if that situation arises, especially in the interest of developing a long and mutually rewarding relationship, but that in the meantime and given the state of the law, it is simply not right of them to demand it of you and, as a prudent businessperson, you cannot agree to it.

On the other hand, if your business rarely employs a lawyer or doesn't face much legal action, or if this is a small matter you are dealing with and you feel strongly that this is the best lawyer for you, the clause may not be worth dying on the sword for.

As in other areas of life, your judgment—and counsel from a caring attorney looking out for your best interest—will save the day.

IN REAL LIFE

Sylvester works at Foghorn Big Law Firm. Bugs & Co. retains him for tax advice. Meanwhile, Yosemite Samsonite Inc. wants to hire Foghorn Big Law Firm to sue Bugs & Co. for a breach of contract completely unrelated to the tax advice Sylvester gives Bugs & Co. Law firms are typically restricted from acting for Yosemite Samsonite Inc. without the express permission from both Bugs & Co. and Yosemite Samsonite Inc. for the obvious reason that sensitive information about each company can be used by the other in many different permutations.

Foghorn Big Law Firm doesn't want to pass up the fees associated with its representation of Yosemite Samsonite Inc. But even getting the consent itself invokes sensitive confidentiality and duty of loyalty rules that are difficult to get around.

The Moral

Just like Bugs & Co. and Yosemite Samsonite Inc. will be in a far better position to decide if they wish to grant a conflict waiver at the time the issue becomes relevant and not before, so will you.

Other

Most jurisdictions at least recommend the use of an engagement agreement. Be sure your lawyer walks you through its terms, and if they say something like, "Rules of professional conduct require that I include that information," get in the habit of asking for the specific reference. More than a few lawyers have relied on that excuse, but it may or may not apply. It's up to you to verify that.

Remember that lawyers will sometimes recommend that you have your own lawyer just to help you through the engagement letter. Despite how obscene this situation is, know that you also have that option.

THE FIGS RIPE FOR NEGOTIATING

As we discussed in the previous chapter, you can use your negotiating power to improve the quality of your engagement with your lawyer.

Fees and conflicts are two figs already ripe for negotiating consideration. But the smaller, less ripe figs are those that you highlight as being relevant to your particular situation or business. That's why reading with a critical eye rather than with cute, half-asleep doggie eyes is critical to this process. Cute isn't going to save you money—at least here.

Sometimes you just need a few good ideas to stimulate your creativity in finding places to negotiate. With that in mind, I invite you to write to me and tell me about your successes *and* failures in doing so. If appropriate and with your permission, I'll add to the already assembled resources at manageyourlawyer.com/negotiate.

Rather than empty statements, we can *act* and, together, become stronger.

USE BIG COMPANY GUIDELINES

The recent COVID-19 pandemic saw the little guy sacrificed in favor of big corporate and political powerhouses. It's long past time that braver elements of society take better advantage of the benefits flowing to those bigger players.

Many big companies develop their own guidelines for use of outside counsel.

These guidelines include things like:

- Not billing for summer students or young associates at meetings.

- Not billing for firm overhead, including things like photocopies, postage, secretarial services, or meals for lawyers working overtime.

- Requiring approval before an expert or another counsel is hired.

- Requiring alternative billing arrangements.

Is there any reason smaller companies can't ask for the same accommodations? Assuming the approach is appropriate, no.

But will a law firm agree to those accommodations from anyone other than a big company?

Enterprising and creative small businesses have found greater freedom to create their own destinies and there's nothing wrong with trying. I won't mislead you and suggest you are *likely* to be successful in getting those accommodations. That depends largely on you and the work you bring to a law firm. But imagine if every business was respected enough by their lawyers to take reasonable and fair requests for accommodations seriously. This is all that I am proposing throughout this book.

And just imagine if every small business in America acted on the ideas and suggestions in this book. The power structure would be very different. Lawyers may claim that the industry would never let it happen. But other than for the largest of law firms that feed off big corporate clientele, that is not a dependable argument. These are issues we'll touch on more when we discuss ALSPs in Chapter 9.

Sometimes we need to be that first brave person. The leader. The single voice that will inspire others. That is what leadership is. There's nothing brave about following the mob.

Show yourself to be a desirable client, and ask nicely, with strength and conviction. You don't need to be a big bank or firm to be a legitimate business that is highly attractive to a law firm. You don't need to be big at all to negotiate successfully.

SYSTEM SUGGESTIONS

In the Preliminary Steps area of your project management tool, create a folder called Engagement Letter, and upload a copy of it there. Create a checklist of items within that folder, including:

- Read the engagement letter.

- Put the terms in language I understand.

- Identify the parts I do not understand and/or the parts I have concerns with.

- Set up a meeting with my lawyer to discuss questions and negotiation points.

For examples of what this might look like in practice, scan the QR code below or visit manageyourlawyer.com/engagement.

CHAPTER 7

RETAINERS ARE A SPECIAL KIND OF PRIVILEGE

IMAGINE A LAWYER SAYS TO YOU, "ACCOUNTANTS, DOCTORS, lawyers—we all make mistakes. No one is perfect. We all know that. But we ask for a retainer because we have a duty to give clients the best representation possible."[28]

---

28 Inspiration for this mock quote is taken from Scott Adams, *Win Bigly: Persuasion in a World Where Facts Don't Matter* (New York: Portfolio/Penguin, 2017).

These are two persuasion techniques strung together. The first is called the "high-ground maneuver," which was inspired by Steve Jobs when he masterfully deflected criticism away from the glitch in the iPhone 4 that caused calls to drop just by holding the phone a certain way.

In the press conference in which he did that, on July 10, 2010, Jobs addressed the criticism over the iPhone 4, saying, "You know...we're not perfect. We know that, you know that, and ahhh...phones aren't perfect, either. But we want to make it, make all of our users happy. However we started getting some reports of people having issues with the antenna system, which is a very advanced new antenna system... doesn't seem like a good idea if you can touch your phone or more in particular grip your phone in a certain way and the bars go way down, that doesn't seem like a good thing. Well it turns out, it's certainly not unique to the iPhone 4. That was one of the first things we learned. You could go on YouTube and see videos of Nokia phones and Motorola phones and other phones doing the same thing, nobody had ever looked at 'em much before but I think it's important to understand the scope of this

For anyone who's paid a lawyer's retainer as a condition for the lawyer starting to work for you, you know this is essentially what the lawyer says to you. "You pay for the work first. Then we work. It's necessary, and it's for your own good—and it's just the way it is."

Dream job. Cash flow problems a thing of the distant past.

It's also how lawyers have normalized retainers in a way that many other industries have not. Moreover, many lawyers claim retainers are a way to develop trust, not taketh it away.

---

problem because what the data says leads you to the conclusion that this has been blown so out of proportion that it's...it's incredible. So let me tell you what we're going to do..."

Jobs goes on to describe some fixes and giveaways. (His remarks can be found via CNET here: "Steve Jobs on iPhone 4 Fixes," CNET, YouTube Video, 2:25, July 16, 2010, https://www.youtube.com/watch?v=2ZctdV9dZyE.)

Scott Adams describes the persuasion Jobs used here to change the argument from "the iPhone 4 has problems" to "all smartphones have problems." This is an example of what he calls the "high-ground maneuver," or saying something true about a bigger-picture issue such that a critic who wants to pull the conversation back to the smaller issue will "fear appearing small-minded if they drag the argument back to the detail level" (Win Bigly, 196).

Scott Adams also describes another persuasion technique he refers to as the "fake because." Adams claims using a "because" with someone who needs a little push to agree with you gives them "permission" to buy your argument.

In the case of retainers, what client would want a push in the direction of the thing they don't want to do (i.e., pay the retainer)? I'd argue that it's effective here because clients are already primed to pay a retainer and it is easier to do what is expected of them rather than have to get into a negotiation about whether the retainer is appropriate or not.

The example I've provided may not be the best example of the high-ground maneuver or the fake because. The beautiful thing about persuasion is that it doesn't always have to be that good to be effective. A lawyer saying this to a client (which in essence they have done in the course of normalizing the retainer requirement) makes it very difficult for a client to fight back—unless that client appreciates that any normalized behavior can be renormalized, which is why I have spent several paragraphs here going into it.

When I addressed this topic in the first ever How Not To Get Screwed By Your Lawyer Workshop™, one of the attendees—the decades-long owner of a large business in one of America's largest cities—openly queried how different his business life might be if his industry normalized advance payment as a matter of course.

Another workshop attendee asked, "Who put them on a pedestal?"

It was an entertaining few minutes as the participants aired their grievances and wondered openly if arguments for advance payments could be made in other industries that have *not* normalized retainers. It's understandable. The inherent nature of a retainer, which guarantees payment to the lawyer, assumes a client will act badly (i.e., not pay) before there is any evidence of such bad behavior. It's also very inconsistent with one of the most fundamental tenets of the law: that you are innocent until proven guilty.

But we're back to backward.

As commonly understood, the retainer is an advance payment for services to be rendered. That sum is deposited into a trust account on behalf of the client and controlled by the attorney or law firm, and it guarantees payment to the attorney for work performed.

The funds become earned once the lawyer has performed work for the client and the lawyer has sent an invoice for that work, at which point the lawyer may transfer the amount represented in the invoice from the client's trust account into the lawyer's operating account.

Even better for the lawyer, it's often a condition of the legal relationship that the lawyer not be obliged to do any further work until retainers are replenished. You saw an example of this wording in Chapter 6 on engagement letters.

These inherent realities create friction in an oft-strained relationship between lawyer and client, exacerbated by the knowledge that lawyers don't have to ask for a retainer. The request for a retainer will come off as "I'm excited to work for you! But I don't trust that you'll pay your bill, so you need to pay me first. I don't ask all my clients to pay a retainer, but I'm asking you."

Between engagement letters and retainers, there's little wonder the lawyer-client relationship fits about as well as Cinderella's shoe on an ugly stepsister.

To be fair to our friendly lawyers, though, it's also easy to imagine how challenging it is for lawyers to get paid when clients are unhappy with the lawyer's work or a legal result, which may be the case even when a lawyer does the best job that can be done. For as many bad lawyers as there may be, there are certainly bad clients and those who do not pay their bills make it more expensive for everyone.[29]

Furthermore, some might argue that a lawyer should be compensated as soon as the relationship begins because the use of a law firm's or lawyer's name may be enough to spark movement from the other side. For example, a dispute with your neighbor is easier to blow off before you get a formal lawyer's

---

29 Bad client behavior making things more expensive for everyone is true in most industries, isn't it?

letter on behalf of your annoying neighbor who isn't happy that a few overhanging branches are dropping acorns on their manicured lawn.

Specialized expertise, particularly in a jurisdiction where such expertise is less common, may be another common justification for requesting a retainer.

It's hard to say therefore whether the retainer is an archaic relic that we continue to tolerate, like New York City real estate brokers for rentals or big government politicians who profit off division of citizenship, or if retainers are a good way to align a lawyer's interests with their clients, as all good arrangements should strive to do.[30]

And that perhaps is the most important point here. Consider that either paying or not paying a retainer is another opportunity to guide your lawyer to align their interests to yours. Because of this and since the industry has at the present time normalized retainers, the rest of this chapter will explore the features of retainers that may or may not serve you and a simple process for better managing them.

UNCAPED CRUSADERS: BAR ASSOCIATIONS

Lawyer-governing bodies don't like it when lawyers dive into trust funds, and a lawyer's drinking, gambling, or any other

---

30 Either way, the good thing about "normalized" behavior is that it can be renormalized in the opposite fashion. So whichever way you see it, it's likely to work out for you at some point in time.

problem that makes it more likely a lawyer will dive in for personal use is no excuse. Other than a failure to pay bar dues, abuse of a client's trust fund is commonly regarded as one of the few things that evokes truly serious penalties.

Although each bar association has a system to discipline bad actors with penalties ranging from suspension to fines to disbarment, like with all large bureaucratic organizations, these things take time. Too much time. How long before someone finds out and then reports are written, investigations started and finished, hearings scheduled, decisions rendered, and appeals exhausted?

A lawyer who steals from a client's trust fund is unlikely to do it just once before he dips his hand back in the double chocolate chunk cookie jar. Yet it could take years before a lawyer will be disciplined or taken out of circulation from an unsuspecting public.[31]

IN REAL LIFE

Fatima is Chester's criminal lawyer. He paid her a large lump sum. At Fatima's instruction, he also signed a power of attorney granting power to one of her staff members to ensure some of those funds would be used to settle his obligations while he served time in prison. After time served, Chester was released and found his property absconded, including the entirety of the tens of thousands

---

31 Although many lawyers carry malpractice insurance to cover such losses, many do not. Only two states—Oregon and Idaho—require lawyers to carry it. More and more states are considering making malpractice insurance mandatory.

of dollars initially deposited in the trust account, and the POA requirements unfulfilled.

Fatima claimed that all the trust funds were for the purpose of Chester's defense (a mere few hours of subpar work). There was no sign of the staff member or the property that was the subject of the POA. Chester filed a bar complaint, and after months of waiting for the hearing date, all the while living rather destitute, the case came before the disciplinary committee—only after the committee had taken in at least four other complaints spanning the course of several years, and only to be delayed further the week of the original hearing date at Fatima's request.

It took years of a corrupt lawyer absconding with client funds before the disciplinary committee reprimanded Fatima. There was no recourse to the cheated clients. Fatima had poor, money-sucking habits and was not in a position to satisfy debts, even if Chester had been willing to pursue a burdensome civil suit against her and would have been successful.

The Moral

A bad lawyer disciplined or even stripped of their license is of little comfort to a client who has been screwed by their attorney. That bar associations take so long (and possibly even address so few matters of misconduct, relatively speaking) adds insult to injury.

In the brilliant if not stolen words of Shakespeare, "There's the rub!" Because even when a lawyer is sanctioned by bar associations (or equivalent lawyer-governing bodies), the pillaged client gets nothing. If the disciplinary committee lays down a punishment that will actually dissuade the lawyer from repeating the bad behavior and potentially prevent future abuse of the public, the complaining client can at least have that comfort.[32] Otherwise, the disciplinary process is no more effective than having a breakup conversation for "closure." No one gets closure from those awkward conversations, just like no one gets any real closure (or recourse) from a lawyer facing disciplinary committee sanctions.

DIFFERENT RETAINERS FOR DIFFERENT FOLKS

A retainer for services to be rendered differs from a type of retainer that goes by different names—a "pure," "case," "availability," or "general" retainer.

The main difference is that the retainer is paid to ensure the lawyer is available for a designated period of time, or as an advance to ensure the lawyer is not retained by clients that may be adversarial to the person paying the retainer. For

---

32 Omahkohkiaaiipooyii, "The Art of Getting Disbarred for Perjury," So That the Peoples May Live, December 19, 2013, https://sttpml.org/the-art-of-getting-disbarred-for-perjury/.

As a decades-long lawyer wrote under the pen name Roger Rabbit in 2013, "There are only two things a lawyer can be absolutely certain will get him/her disbarred: Steal from your clients or, even worse, fail to pay your bar dues. The latter is the most serious conceivable offense and will get a lawyer suspended within 31 days, guaranteed, with permanent disbarment sure to follow..."

It's hard to discern if this article is tongue-in-cheek or real. It sure seems real. Anyone authoring an article under the name Roger Rabbit is worth some time. Check out the reference and you can make up your own mind. Maybe we should discuss this over drinks. Join me at manageyourlawyer.com/funny for the dog-and-pony show that is "lawyerly governance."

example, let's suppose you own a successful specialty grocery store. Gossip along the grapevine is that a national brand with a well-known expansion plan has set its sights on your jurisdiction. You might pay a general retainer to a reputable corporate transactional firm to ensure they are available to represent you over the next six months in the event a deal starts to percolate.

The names given to retainers are not used consistently or are used interchangeably. The language is not important. It is the *terms* of the retainer that matter (terms that will be explained in an engagement letter—another reason to read it).

When you read it, ask yourself the following questions:

- Is the retainer nonrefundable or are there terms on refundability?

- Must it be replenished, and if so, when and on what conditions?

- How is the retainer credited against the lawyer's work?

- Is the lawyer part of a larger firm with a greater number of gatekeepers on trust funds, lowering the risk that trust funds will disappear?

NEGOTIATING THE RETAINER

The only reasonable retainer may be one where you don't already have a relationship with the attorney, in an amount representative of the number of hours or amount of work that is expected for the file.

If you're being asked to pay a retainer that you think is unreasonable or that you are not 100 percent clear about, ask the lawyer about it, and suggest a path that you think is more appropriate (keeping in mind your desire to align your collective interests).

Most often, retainers should also be refundable. Lawyers will sometimes claim once the money is in trust, it's no longer the client's money. You should take the view that it's your money until earned; otherwise, you might be tempted to see the retainer as a sunk cost before it actually becomes one (that issue is discussed later in this chapter).

RETAINERS IN CRIMINAL LAW: HIGHER PROBABILITY THAT YOU'RE SCREWED

Hopefully, this entire section is irrelevant for your purposes, but it is instructive for illustrating a different context for retainers.

Lawyers will find ways to bill you and say, "You've got a great case and you should fight, fight, fight!" until you can no longer pay them or granny's done gone and gave away all her land so there's nothing more to convey on your behalf. (See, for example, the "In Real Life" example in Chapter 12.)

The ABA doesn't help, as we know from reading Comment 5 to Rule 1.5 in their Rules of Professional Conduct:[33]

> [5] An agreement may not be made whose terms might induce the lawyer improperly to curtail services for the client or perform them in a way contrary to the client's interest. For example, a lawyer should not enter into an agreement whereby services are to be provided only up to a stated amount when it is foreseeable that more extensive services probably will be required, unless the situation is adequately explained to the client. Otherwise, the client might have to bargain for further assistance in the midst of a proceeding or transaction. However, it is proper to define the extent of services in light of the client's ability to pay. A lawyer should not exploit a fee arrangement based primarily on hourly charges by using wasteful procedures.

It's hard to understand how this squares with the reality, particularly in the seedy underworld of criminal defense work, which has a lawyer taking a deposited sum of, say, $50,000—and then perhaps dragging out a deal with a prosecutor that could have been made on day one. Instead, the lawyer decided to take it to day X minus 1—where X is the day the retainer runs out.

---

33 "Rule 1.5, Fees—Comment," American Bar Association, August 16, 2018, https://www.americanbar.org/groups/professional_responsibility/publications/model_rules_of_professional_conduct/rule_1_5_fees/comment_on_rule_1_5/.

What is to be done? How do you argue that's what's happened, let alone prove it? And how does another lawyer or prosecutor even call that out?

These are the types of situations that are hard to control. It's best to avoid them entirely, to the extent possible, or at least attempt to negotiate down any large retainer, recognizing the reality that if a lawyer takes money up front, you're unlikely to get a refund for portions "unused."

RECONCILE YOUR BILL TO YOUR TRUST ACCOUNT

At least the rules governing lawyers' maintenance of trust accounts are strict. Lawyers are under strict fiduciary obligations to ensure a client's trust account is maintained separately from the lawyer's property, in the jurisdiction in which the client is located, and with complete and accurate accounting.

Like any bad situation in life, it's better to avoid the trouble in the first place. No matter how strict, lawyers still abscond with trust assets.

Here are a few steps to avoid trouble, or at least bring it to light sooner than further down the drain:

1. Review your engagement letter and understand the discrete and straightforward terms associated with your account. For example, is the retainer refundable or nonrefundable, and if the latter, for

what purpose? Does the retainer account need to be replenished, and how often? What are the payment terms? How often will a bill be rendered?

2. Review your bills as soon as you receive them (more on this in Chapter 10).

3. Do a reconciliation of your bill to your trust account. Depending on the complexity of your legal matter, this may be nothing more than ensuring the amount deducted from your trust account is the amount reflected on your bill. Regardless, this is certainly nothing more complicated than any other number of financial metrics you need to monitor in your business. Whether simple errors or negligence, it's money, and it needs to be monitored.

The key in all this is to ensure you approach your retainer as your money, which we alluded to early on in this chapter. Now let's finish the thought because it is perhaps the most important issue.

THE RETAINER IS NOT A SUNK COST

Another of my workshop attendees made the obvious but important observation that if there's $50,000 in a retainer, lawyers will come up with a way to invoice $50,000. Although lawyers are bound by ethics not to request a retainer in an amount greater than the expected cost for services (as noted above), this hardly amounts to any real protection for the client.

The fact remains that the retainer often acts as an advance on payment, and like any deposit, there's some measure of risk involved in protecting it.

There is something about a deposit that makes it *feel* like a sunk cost. It's why you will buy a no-refund ticket and still not show up on occasion. It's why a gift card—no matter how much we know that it represents cash—doesn't *feel* the same as cash. Although there are plenty of examples in the real world of a deposit becoming a legitimate sunk cost, it's rare that a retainer should ever feel like a sunk cost, and most certainly not through the normal progression of your legal matter.

Yes, I know you know better: you're not about to let a retainer go to waste and will not just accept whatever bill comes at you. But can I ask you something?

How often do you carefully review your medical bills? Phone bills? Credit card statements? Especially when they are subject to automatic payments.

So you don't need to tell me that you don't always read your legal bills with the gusto that function deserves. It's okay. I know. We all know.

Just recognizing that you have, in the past, treated a retainer as a sunk cost might help you question whether you need to blindly accept the next request you get for a retainer. And where you do pay a retainer, you'll know to create a better system around what you should be doing instead, including reconciling your bill to your trust account.

Sometimes a shift in mindset will make a world of difference.

SYSTEM SUGGESTIONS

Create a folder for Trust Account, and upload any separate retainer agreements here (if separate from your engagement letter). Include steps one to three (from Reconcile Your Bill to Your Trust Account) in a checklist and build out additional processes to ensure those items are completed.

CHAPTER 8

THE LAWYER-SAVING MAGIC OF BILLING PRACTICES

IN AMERICA, HOW MUCH DO PEOPLE SPEND ON LEGAL fees every year?

A. $25 billion

B. $43 billion

C. $87 billion

D. $100 billion

Answer: D. One hundred *billion* dollars. It almost seems criminal that I can get to Chapter 8 without diving into that money. But here we are.

Remember the 1993 legal thriller *The Firm*, based on John Grisham's novel? The highest-grossing R-rated movie of that year made business heads spin. Yes, it was just a movie, but what businessperson wasn't thinking, *Am I getting screwed like all those clients?*

The passage of time may make us feel more evolved as a human species, but when it comes to legal billing practice, it's hard to say whether we've evolved as much as we think. Those pesky incentive structures sure haven't changed any.

In this chapter, we're going to be delving into everyone's favorite topic: money. We'll review billing mechanics and reveal a few of the elephants in the lobby. Because when it comes to billing, there are so many elephants we might as well be in the Serengeti. Elephants largely travel as a matriarchal family, so we will travel as they do here in this chapter.

The issue isn't that we're looking for fraud in the way of *The Firm*. Rather, we need only highlight a reality of human behavior that even well-meaning and thoughtful people ignore.

Where incentives to cheat are high, the number of people involved big, the chance of getting caught low, and the repercussions of getting caught minimal in comparison to the gain, it is naive and dumb to think cheating will not happen. Whether there is "no evidence!" does not determine the reality. Surely, we can all remember from our undergraduate course in logic that the absence of evidence for XYZ does not mean that XYZ does not exist.

the fiduciary obligations we hold to clients—and
mportantly than that, that it does nothing to truly
ons between lawyers and clients, and it allows this
awyers to continue.

rld devolves into paying millions of dollars for
e papers by experts who are consistently wrong on
ble scale, I have to wonder, what if we could better
l problems?

ve a better alternative at the moment, so I would put a
tion like this on the table:

respect your work and want to work with you. I'm not
asking for these billing accommodations because I'm trying
to make your life difficult but because it's necessary for my
business. I know how easy it is for legal fees to get out of
control, and I know that's not your fault and comes down
to the complicated and bureaucratic system that you have
to help me get through. What I don't want to happen is
that I've made these stipulations thinking we now have an
open and honest relationship, only to find that the hours
are showing up elsewhere. So if as time goes on you feel
there's something in these accommodations that no longer
works for you and your firm, I'd much rather we discuss it,
and to the extent I understand your position and we need
to change that billing policy, I will be more than happy to
discuss and entertain that. I'm looking forward to a long-
term relationship with you and would like to discuss issues
like this openly.

After hiring and firing three money "managers" over the
years, I now trade stocks on my own behalf. I don't need to
see "evidence!" of insider trading to know it's happening.
Every day.

And yet, perversions of this basic rule of logic have been, are,
and will continue to be used to pit good and smart people
against other good and smart people until the end of time. It
does a great disservice to us all.

Such is life. Keep a smile on your face. And your hands clean.

This discussion matters to our elephants.

ELEPHANT OVERVIEW

Fees are generally one of three types:

1. **Hourly:** A set wage per hour and per person.

2. **Fixed:** A flat fee for all or a portion of your matter.
   Fixed or flat fees are generally used in cases
   involving criminal, divorce, custody, or bankruptcy
   issues. They're also often used for drafting particular
   types of standard documents like wills or trusts.

3. **Contingency:** The lawyer receives a percentage of
   the amount you receive via settlement. These are
   more typical when there is a potentially large payout,
   such as in a personal injury matter or other litigation.

This is not an exhaustive list because creative billing arrangements continue to respond to a more sophisticated clientele and an increasingly competitive landscape. We'll touch on a few alternative structures at the end of this chapter.

MOMMA ELEPHANT

Here's the biggest problem and I'll tell you right up front I don't have a solid solution. But I have to believe that, as this problem we're going to discuss momentarily is given more airtime, and more lawyers understand that clients understand it, better relationships will emerge, by (1) pure force of good and more lawyers looking at themselves in the mirror and condemning the practice, (2) a more efficient legal system that uncovers unscrupulous billing practices through better and more readily available technology including for clients that are not big clientele, or (3) some combination of the first two. My vote is with (3), and I think it's already happening.

While we're waiting for this to manifest into a better overall system and better world, you need to be aware of it and explore ways to fix it in your own world.

Enough procrastinating.

Here's the deal. You've asked your lawyer all the right questions and have had an open dialogue. He agrees to a number of billing stipulations:

- No administrative tasks other than by nonbillable staff.

- Limits on internal
- Limits on the numb
- No overhead costs inc library services, trans

You feel good. Like a winner. *I* you're supposed to do. Your law items, but you explained reasor to you and your business, and l work with you.

All the while, your lawyer is thinkir make sure I don't write off any tim or I'll just slip in an extra hour of rate, and it will easily make up for making me agree to.

That's the reality. We don't need "pro to know it's true. Otherwise, good law might wonder how they can take more part they play in the sometimes absurd w rest of the lawyers reading this are sayin And when we look at the other technique rest of the elephant family, you'll see how this problem is to deal with.

Be this as it may, how do we then claim we'r

My hope (albeit naive) is that more and mor comfortable with this approach. That there is

wrong with even more i build relati distrust of l

As the w vapid whi a remarka attack rea

I don't ha conversa

Of course it's naive—says the world telling me I should listen to a teenager with braids and no scientific background raking in millions for impassioned speeches on scientific topics.

And sure, some lawyers might laugh at this type of conversation over a ribeye with their other lawyer friends. Many others will appreciate the vulnerability and feel even greater responsibility toward their clients.

After all, what deal does not require a good measure of trust between the parties—no matter how tight and locked up the legal documentation? If we are truly trying to create a better world—and we should be because the alternative stinks—then being a model for more honest and open negotiation is not naive.

In addition to being an attractive client (see Chapter 5), there's one *really* big thing on the good guy's side here. Absent more fundamental changes to the highly politicized justice system, none of which I foresee coming, the competitive landscape will become more intense, not less. As competitiveness intensifies, these conversations could become even more powerful.

For forward-thinking lawyers and law firms, there is a golden marketing opportunity here, and it might also be a highly profitable way to combat the ever-growing, low-cost DIY service providers like LegalZoom, LegalShield, and Rocket Lawyer, which do not directly rely on relationship building (at least in some part).

Even when you can't tell for sure if this game is what your lawyer is doing, you may get a sense of whether it is happening. Remember in the book *Blink* how Malcolm Gladwell[34] started off talking about an art expert being able to just look at a piece of art and, without being able to articulate why, declare it a fraud?

Admittedly, this is a tough one, as even Gladwell acknowledges where it can go wrong. Ultimately, we can leave this debate alone since we can at least agree we have intuition of some sort. And whether in business or in your personal life, you know where it's guided you and where it hasn't.

Be confident in your intuition, but keep an open mind too. Balance being guarded and suspicious with a desire for a good relationship.

POPPA ELEPHANT

Imagine you found a series of entries on your bill that looked like this:

Research; emails; conferences

Swearing under your breath and paying the bill is an option. It's a common result because who wants to go through the trouble of requesting clarification and possibly feeling like

---

34 Malcolm Gladwell, *Blink: The Power of Thinking without Thinking* (New York: Little, Brown, 2005).

an idiot because you don't understand your lawyer's cryptic entries? It's much easier to avoid the insecurity of having to face the "What does this mean?" question going through your mind and the "What a pain in the ass to deal with" devil on your shoulder.

Vague billing practices may not be considered "shady" to some, but they are arguably the shadiest of all. They occur frequently and rely on those insecurities and devils because honestly, who has the time to deal with the incredibly unsexy issue of asking a lawyer to clarify? This is the process of normalizing behavior in action.

The good thing about normalized behavior is that it can be reversed and renormalized. Asking for clarification in these cases is legitimate and desirable. It should be sufficient to ask once and direct your lawyer to provide more detail on the current bill and all future bills. Ideally, that request for sufficient detail should come at the engagement letter stage. But even if you ask, it's possible your lawyer won't follow the rules.

That detail should not be coming at your expense. But how would we know if it were? We end up with a case of Momma Elephant where we won't know for sure if some other time entry was just boosted to make up for the extra half hour or more of time expended in adjusting the legal invoice.

The long and short of it is that vague billing practices are 100 percent unacceptable. We'll deal with this in greater detail in the next chapter.

BABY ELEPHANTS

The Firm may just be a movie from thirty years ago and clients may have grown more sophisticated, but shady law firm practices are alive and well. The legal infrastructure of our society hasn't changed much, other than the availability of ALSPs (that discussion is coming up), so we equally shouldn't expect billing matters to change. Here are a few still-too-common shady activities to be aware of that gumption and this book can combat.

Baby Elephant 1: Obscene Increments

The standard billing increment is one-tenth of an hour. If a lawyer works for five minutes, your bill will reflect 0.1 hours. Unfortunately, there are lawyers who still bill by quarter-hour increments, despite how antiquated this practice has become. So in this example, you'd be billed 0.25 hours.

During my career, a senior lawyer at a competing law firm commented humorously about some of his colleagues who would not think twice about billing every moment of their time, including to clients who called to change a meeting. At $600 an hour and billing in quarter of an hour increments, that's $150 for a two-minute phone call to change a meeting that a secretary could easily have been responsible for.

As shady billing practices go, this one is easy to deal with. Just confirm your lawyer bills by the smallest increment of time (usually one-tenth of an hour, or 0.1) prior to hiring your attorney or ensure it's clearly indicated in the engagement letter. It's worth asking yourself if a lawyer who bills by anything greater than one-tenth increments is someone who could view the client as anything other than a piece of meat.

Serious Kobe beef burger time.

I would go further to suggest that modern technology being what it is, lawyers being paid a tip on every one-tenth hour worked is obscene. It would be one thing if time was rounded down—for example, if seven minutes worked would be billed at 0.1 hours rather than 0.2. And some lawyers do round down. But that happens only on rare occasion, and legal firm billing software typically rounds up. Why shouldn't we be asking why billing is simply not reflected by the minute?

In 2020, we saw Elon Musk's SpaceX coordinate with NASA and forge a new generation of space innovation with the successful launch of the Falcon 9 and Crew Dragon.[35]

And the legal industry twists itself into a pretzel to explain to (what they perceive as) a powerless public that a more precise and fair calculation of billing their clients is "too complicated" by billing anything less than 0.1 hours.

Baby Elephant 2: Block Billing

Instead of recording time for separate tasks, lawyers frequently use block billing to assemble little bits of time into bigger bits of time.

---

35 Sisso Cao, "10 Incredible Photos from NASA and SpaceX's Historic First Human Launch," Observer, June 1, 2020, https://observer.com/2020/06/spacex-nasa-crew-mission-launch-photo-recap/.

There are two main problems with this. First, it is impossible for a client to know how much time went into each particular task, making assessment of the bill more difficult. Second, there are often incentives to round up.

For example, let's suppose your lawyer spends ten minutes responding to your questions via email, ninety minutes drafting a purchase agreement, and eight minutes reviewing a junior lawyer's document.

This would amount to 1.8 hours, and lawyers will often reflect this block of time instead of itemizing the three individual tasks. The final block bill entry might also look like this:

Draft email to client; draft purchase agreement; review escrow agreement = 2 hours.

In isolation, the extra 0.2 hours is insignificant. Multiplied time and time again across any number of lawyers, this is hardly different than what we saw in *The Firm*—and yet, they don't *feel* the same, do they? One has been normalized and accepted right under our noses.

It's disturbing.

In a 2003 study, the California State Bar[36] concluded that the use of block billing inflates a legal bill by 10–30 percent. And even though block billing has been condemned by many courts, it is still typical practice.

---

36 "Detecting Attorney Bill Padding," State Bar of California, January 29, 2003, http://www.calbarjournal.com/Portals/0/documents/mfa/2014/2003-01_Detecting-Atty-Bill-Padding_r.pdf.

Lawyers might argue that charges for legal services should reflect not only the hourly rate but also the value provided to the client and the responsibility borne by the lawyer.

This proposition renders the already obscene hourly billing rate nothing more than a rough estimate. To be sure, engagement letters often provide a blanket statement that bills may reflect these other very obscure notions of value.

Push back against them. The hourly billing rate should already reflect "value to the client" and "responsibility borne by the lawyer." For lawyers using that billing model especially, they should not also demand to eat their peanut butter chocolate cake with loosey-goosey adjustments too.

Baby Elephant 3: Hoarding Hours

Law firms will advertise their ability to "staff appropriately," which means the most junior lawyer or staff capable of doing the work will do it. Except that when times are tight and lawyers' phones eerily quiet, more expensive lawyers keep more of the work than cheaper ones. A partner may do an associate's work. Or a paralegal may do a secretary's work.

This is not cool, particularly among large law firms with a large roster of employees and an entire economic structure designed around the model of choosing appropriate staff.

Common as it may be, catching this one also poses challenges. It's not readily apparent to a client if legal work is appropriately allocated to the right level of lawyer or not. On the other hand, it's not impossible to figure this out, and a prudent client asking a few of the right questions and observing trends could pick up something that doesn't seem right.

Baby Elephant 4: Too Many at the Party

This problem has been happening forever. A client in my How Not To Get Screwed By Your Lawyer Workshop once bemoaned a mediation he was forced to attend prior to commencing litigation. As he looked around the beautiful mediation facility, the scent of fresh-brewed coffee in his nostrils and his colleagues' gluttonous chewing of donuts hitting his eardrums, he wondered why he needed to pay for it all as well as his senior lawyer, who had brought along two junior lawyers and a staff member. The dog-and-pony show dragged on all day, and his frustration grew to a boiling point.

Similarly, I was on a webinar recently where general counsel at a large company in a major financial center complained that his big corporate law firm consistently had been using "too many people" on a matter. It was one of the factors that prompted him to explore the use of ALSPs for some of his needs.

Law firms have successfully passed the cost of training young lawyers on to their clients in a most blatant way. This is another instance where larger companies have in some cases successfully refused to pay for such costs via outside billing guidelines (see Chapter 5).

Rather than letting blood boil, discuss with your lawyer what makes sense. It is often appropriate to have multiple lawyers at a single meeting, depending on how work is allocated, but that is not universally true. When work enters the realm of training, there's no reason the client should be paying for it. Push back.

AN INDICTMENT OF ONE'S OWN PROFESSION?

A colleague made an offer to several different general counsels that I would have thought would never have been refused—except it was.

In the course of various consulting projects for a number of large businesses, my colleague offered to review legal bills of at least $100,000, insisting that he could find at least 3 percent savings. He offered the task at no charge, in conjunction with other work that he had already been hired for.

All general counsels refused the offers. But why? Why would they not be inclined to find a minimum of a few thousand dollars of savings through a simple review of legal bills that would cost them nothing?

General counsel positions are most often filled by lawyers who once worked at law firms. Depending on the size of the company, the general counsel positions often include managing external counsel.

Ensuring their company is not overbilled would seem the most basic of fiduciary obligations that any general counsel would have to their corporate entity.

Would they refuse because they doubted the claim? Unlikely. Would they say that they were capable of raising any issues? Perhaps. What is equally or more likely is that these "give or take" bills are seen as a cost of doing business. Any review—particularly when the general counsel is working with their old firm—could be seen as an indictment of their own management and needless rocking of the boat.

It seems innocent enough, but perhaps not to any number of employees of the company who might need to work a week or a month to make that $3,000. Or to any number of shareholders who rely on the company's best performance for any number of investment reasons.

For readers of this book who are unlikely to have the luxury of general counsel to manage the legal affairs of their businesses, you can equally do a better job than any low-standard general counsel.

We'll deal with that review in Chapter 10.

ALTERNATIVE BILLING ARRANGEMENTS

Creative businesspeople should never shy away from bringing their strategic mindset to the billing-arrangement table. Lawyers and their clientele have continued to evolve alternative billing structures to better address the needs of a changing marketplace, fueled by two primary catalysts: a continuously evolving and sophisticated user of legal services and more entrepreneurial alternative legal service providers (ALSPs). ALSPs need their own chapter, and that is coming up next.

For now, let's briefly touch on some of the more common features of alternative billing arrangements that business users of legal services especially might benefit from.

Flat Fees

Whether it's a car, knee surgery, or legal services for a routine acquisition, not knowing the precise cost of a good or service is frustrating and annoying, and it makes business more challenging.

A common complaint from legal clients is that they never know what the legal bill will be. At the same time, many lawyers like to distinguish themselves as doing "cutting-edge," "bespoke," and "noncommoditized" legal work.

But not all work is unique. For example, some corporate documents, wills, and many time-consuming litigation tasks are routine and do not demand specialized knowledge. Or in the alternative, they may benefit significantly from specialists who can do that work most competently and efficiently. This type of work may be suited to a fixed fee.

The commoditization of legal work has continued unabated, and this has made flat fees more common. While many law firms claim to not want commodity work, there are a lot of large corporate clients with a significant volume of commodity work. Following the financial crisis in 2007–08 in particular, sophisticated clientele requested accommodations in the form of flat fees, and feeling the pinch, big law firms were willing to oblige.

A little research can help you determine if your matter is appropriately suited to flat fees.

Unbundling

The structure of unbundling[37] legal services requires the lawyer to compartmentalize the different legal service needs and offer representation only for certain parts of it. This limited-scope representation improves (at least theoretically) accessibility of justice by providing clients with flexibility, direct expertise in the areas needed, and potentially lower costs.

Unbundling is not appropriate for all matters. But if you are particularly clear about what you need and confident that you can handle the other issues involved, your lawyer may recommend unbundling (or you may wish to ask if it is a suitable option).

Multiple Forms of Payment

You don't need to use only one form of payment. Suppose you'd like to negotiate a fixed fee. Your lawyer resists, bringing up any number of contingencies that could happen. You might find common ground by proposing that a portion of the matter be

37 Stephanie L. Kimbro, "Using Technology to Unbundle in the Legal Services Community," Harvard Journal of Law and Technology Occasional Paper Series, February, 2013, https://papers.ssrn.com/sol3/papers.cfm?abstract_id=2233921; Nicole Black, "Unbundled Legal Services: Steph Kimbro Tells You Everything You Need to Know," MyCase, accessed May 19, 2022, https://www.mycase.com/blog/unbundled-legal-services-steph-kimbro-tells-you-everything-you-need-to-know/. Unbundling is a concept popularized by lawyer and author Stephanie L. Kimbro.

billed on a fixed-fee basis and anything beyond that scope will be billed at a standard hourly rate.

IN REAL LIFE

Geraldine, a real estate developer, and Boris, her lawyer, had worked on several funding deals together. Geraldine approached Boris to request the next deal be done on a fixed-fee basis. Geraldine lamented to me that she got the typical song and dance about "things that might happen" and could not get Boris to agree. She attributed it to Boris's old-timer stodginess and the relatively close-knit market in which they operated. At the time of this writing, Geraldine had not given up proposing alternative billing structures, which Boris might be warming up to. I suspect she will find success in her efforts—a direct result of the relationship she built with her lawyer. Nothing wrong with a little persistence.

The Moral

Depending on your situation, you may be able to come up with a proposal that is enticing to your lawyer and is fully within the bounds of professional conduct.

As frustrating as this chapter may be, understanding billing practices is of obvious importance to managing your legal bills. Furthermore, the better your understanding, the better you can stretch your creative muscle to recommend a suitable and cost-saving alternative billing structure that could work better.

SYSTEM SUGGESTIONS

Plan to have as honest a conversation with your lawyer as you can muster to try and offset the effects of Momma Elephant (where your lawyer may be tempted to stick a few more hours in your bill to make up for any accommodations you've negotiated).

In Chapter 10, we'll discuss reviewing your legal bill. It is in those System Suggestions we'll incorporate the relevant billing tricks covered in this chapter into the appropriate project management folders.

CHAPTER 9

ALTERNATIVE LEGAL SERVICE PROVIDERS: EVOLUTION

KODAK WAS FOUNDED IN 1888 AND BECAME CATEGORY king until financial struggles more than one hundred years later changed its business forever. The name exists, but the model that supports its survival is not like the business it once was.

What dictates the survival or demise of a business? Why did pets.com take an early bust while Chewy founder, Ryan Cohen, sold to PetSmart for $3.35 billion, the largest e-commerce deal in history? Why do some companies buck trends on their way to bankruptcy and others buck harder than a bucking bronco to seemingly endless growth and profit?

The fascinating questions emerging from business case studies tell us about far more than just a bottom line.

What will come of the legal industry?[38] It will continue to adapt and change as it has for hundreds of years.[39] However valid some of the concerns with justice and law firms, most of the big and successful law firms of today will not disappear anytime soon.

That's not necessarily a bad thing for clients and the industry—provided something else emerges to better satisfy the needs of clients for whom big law firms aren't the best answer. ALSPs, also referred to as law companies, are the "something else."

The decision to use an ALSP could alleviate some of the problems you face in trying not to get screwed by your lawyer. So in some ways, this book could have begun with this chapter. On the other hand, understanding if and when it is appropriate to use ALSPs and how they fit into your larger box of screwdrivers along with the other tools in this book will turn you into a Not Screwed rock star.

---

38 David B. Wilkins and Maria Jose Esteban Ferrer, "Taking the 'Alternative' Out of Alternative Legal Service Providers," Harvard Law School, July–August, 2019, https://thepractice.law.harvard.edu/article/taking-the-alternative-out-of-alterna-tive-legal-service-providers/.

Authors David B. Wilkins and Maria Jose Esteban Ferrer describe the flaw in the "alternative" nomenclature, preferring a framework where "legal service providers will be evaluated on their ability to contribute to the creation of real solutions for clients, while also understanding their obligation to help preserve the core values of the rule of law that create the infrastructure that makes every solution, private or public, possible." Although I agree with their premise, to help the reader make clearer distinctions and consider alternatives they may not have already considered, I'll use "ALSPs" to distinguish from traditional law firms.

39 And in even more recent decades, the oversupply of attorneys and technology developments have perhaps taken the "profession" to "trade."

THE DIFFERENCE BETWEEN AN ALSP
AND A LAW FIRM

Typically, someone needing legal services will consider the traditional options:

1. Retain a big, established law firm.

2. Retain a smaller firm or sole practitioner without a big-city presence.

3. DIY.

4. Don't do it at all.

For many reasons already scattered throughout this book like a wildflower seed during a Midwestern tornado season, option one is simply not viable and makes sense only when transactions and matters are of a size and scope capable of justifying the expense of a large law firm. Option two *could* be suitable but is often unable to deliver the specialized service that a client needs. And when a law firm purports to have expertise that they don't really have, the client ends up paying through the nose. Because many people fear the costs and headaches of working with a lawyer, they go for options three or four. Both of those can be dangerous.

It is often the case that all the traditional options suck for everyone other than the larger corporate and institutional clients. For everyone else, including the thousands of smaller businesses that desperately need more efficient delivery of legal services, the ways of big law don't satisfy client needs.

ALSPs may provide a better answer[40] because they offer specialized services through more efficient use of technology and a lower overhead, which means more flexible client solutions, expanding the limited realm of options.

Think of law firms as the heavy-bodied, ever-so-slow giant tortoises that inhabit the Galapagos Islands and ALSPs as the quick, agile, and cunning red fox populations that inhabit every continent other than Antarctica, with continuing healthy populations depending on their environments. ALSPs direct their energies into people and technology capable of delivering more specialized and flexible service with less overhead cost.

The founder of a growing ALSP in Canada summed up the difference this way: "Whereas traditional law firms are structured economically and systemically to the benefit of the partner or lawyer, ALSPs are structured to the benefit of the client."[41]

Whether an industry can continue to grow with a historically systemic misalignment in favor of the provider is debatable and dependent on many factors. It's true that law firms have had no problem growing for decades or centuries. But at some breaking point, perhaps where that point intersects with technology,

---

40   Even where a big law firm services a big corporate client, there are still lots of ALSP opportunities. In fact, law firms account for a significant percentage of the ALSP market. Regardless, even if Big Law continues to exist in its current form, what *is* in all likelihood going to continue to change in that world is the number and size of those firms.

41   Steven Monk, founder of CEOLaw, Toronto, Canada, https://www.ceolawcanada.com/. Note that even if ALSPs do structure themselves to the benefit of the client, ALSPs still benefit in much the same way lawyers and law firms do when people have legal problems, as discussed in Chapter 2.

clients may demand something different. That something may have less and less to do with art-lined walls in pretentious halls. If so, ALSPs will continue to grow in the face of those changing trends, while at least some law firms will wilt.

Alternative or not,[42] future trends or not, in researching for this book and speaking to dozens of business owners along the way, I found that the general public's understanding of ALSPs seems poor, including among regular users of legal services.

That could be because in defining what is an ALSP, many observers lazily prefer to define them by simply rattling off the types of work they do. Something like, "ALSPs provide specialized services like document review, intellectual property management, investigative support, litigation support, and discovery or e-discovery."

That's a good start, but ALSPs can hardly pave the way to the future if too many businesses don't fully appreciate how they can and should be used.

I propose an equally lazy but more customer-friendly, holistic definition: ALSPs are service providers that can potentially get your legal work done faster and cheaper than law firms because they better align incentives to use technology and specialized professionals in favor of the client.

I'm hopeful this chapter will assist the many excellent ALSPs out there working as fast as they can to educate the public and provide more legal services options to them.

---

42 A Thomson Reuters report suggests the nomenclature "alternative legal service providers" should be replaced with "law companies" since trends have made them less "alternative."

A final note: the success of any ALSP depends on the ability of its personnel to deliver quality service. This is no different than the demands on any other business, including traditional law firms themselves. So long as ALSPs are able to attract quality talent, there's no reason to expect they can't do that. While there are many lawyers who seek the prestige and pay of Big Law, there are also many lawyers for whom that gets old. Lawyers are often described as an unhappy group, and the pickings for quality talent are ripe, especially for increasing numbers who seek greater work flexibility.

Technology

ALSPs tend to be defined by their superior adoption of technology and their ability to harness specialized large-scale work, where lawyers do not necessarily have a competitive advantage.

But why is this the case?[43] If an ALSP can do it, why can't a law firm? The answers bring clarity to the distinction between law firms and ALSPs.

First, there's a structural impediment and natural disincentive for law firms to invest in technology. It's not enough to say that

---

43 In addition to the two reasons given here, a Chambers 2021 report on ALSPs points out that law firms do not effectively implement or integrate technologies in the way ALSPs tend to. (One can only assume that the failure to effectively implement and integrate technology will not yield cost savings to the firm, which will therefore not yield cost savings to their clients.) Using an ALSP helps law firms avoid the costs and risks associated with technology acquisition, selection, implementation, and integration. I have no reason to doubt this conclusion, although I believe it still begs the question of why an ALSP uses technology better than a traditional law firm. To download the report, visit https://chambers.com/legal-guide/alternative-legal-service-providers-94/download.

law firms, burdened with big overhead, are generally slower to adopt new technology. They are. But more than that, making large capital investments in better technology that makes client delivery of legal services more effective will not resonate convincingly with partners and lawyers who directly benefit from less efficiency and suffer from a large capital investment.

ALSPs are not typically burdened by those limitations. They have evolved as business first, law second. Unlike with a law firm, an ALSP's competitive advantage may lie, at least in part, in its better use of technology.

Second, law firms will often use technology to support the work product and internal efficiencies that don't necessarily pass their benefits on to clients. For example, a law firm may use enhanced billing software to make it easier for lawyers to bill clients. In contrast, an ALSP may use technology that allows the client to track their lawyer's activity and account balances, which allows the client to address questions or concerns in near real time. This enhances transparency in work product and billing. The ALSP's focus, therefore, is on using technology to improve the relationship with the client.

CONVERGING NEEDS

There is an interesting convergence[44] of demands that might drive the need for ALSPs. Leadership teams at smaller businesses have always had to manage a lot of business functions, from marketing to finance to data management. In recent years, the demands on law departments to broaden their skillset is also growing, at least at bigger companies that have law departments. Historically, those legal departments dealt with strictly legal functions like contracts, litigation, transactions, and intellectual property matters affecting their businesses. The demands on those departments have grown significantly to include many other practice areas like data privacy, risk management, ethics, investor relations, and business continuity. They are also often expected to run as a profitable business unit within the company, enlisting any number of other professional skillsets.

The demand for ALSPs may be further fueled by the convergence of needs among large corporate clients and smaller corporates.

"Are we even doing law?" an ambitious young lawyer turned to me to ask this during a transaction in our early years. A lot of

---

44 A Thomson Reuters report, "In-House Counsel Skills to Support Emerging Law Department Responsibilities," found in its Practical Law service (marked "Maintained") discusses the historic versus modern demands on in-house legal teams that I reflect in this paragraph. https://uk.practicallaw.thomson-reuters.com/w-018-8798?originationContext=knowHow&transitionType=KnowHowItem&contextData=(sc.Default)&firstPage=true.

With respect to my broader point that we see a converging of needs in different markets (i.e., in-house counsel and small businesses without legal teams), I'd be interested in hearing thoughts on whether you agree with my point or not, and if so, why you do or don't think it is relevant to the demand for ALSPs. Write to me at daniela@danielaliscio.com.

legal work is not legal. And yet, legal fees continue to skyrocket, bringing along with them higher fees for law firm tasks that don't require specialized legal expertise but expertise of a different sort—expertise that ALSPs may be better equipped and cheaper to provide than law firms.

DIFFERENT TYPES OF ALSPS

ALSPs are as vast in number and description as dogs in a shelter. I've categorized them below in a way to provide examples of how they might be used for your purposes. For more examples and case studies (which I'd love to hear more of, so write to me!), visit manageyourlawyer.com/ALSP or scan the QR code below:

ALSPs Organized as Law Firms

ALSPs that deliver legal services organize themselves as licensed law firms to comply with requirements against the unauthorized practice of law. They are full-service legal providers and usually provide a large roster of lawyers to fulfill their advertised purpose. Because they have adopted a "client first" model, they differ from a traditional law firm in the way we described in the preceding sections.

For example, a Toronto-based ALSP, CEO Law, is organized as a law firm offering general counsel and specialized services mostly in corporate commercial areas. The company offers tiered services, starting with a DIY model that gives you the option to purchase standard documents, with the ability to add in some cursory help or full board legal assistance at its higher end. Even with full service and no matter how many years of experience the lawyer working on the matter has, hourly rates do not exceed a defined amount. Rates are typically far lower than those charged at traditional law firms in the jurisdictions in which they operate.

Because this ALSP structure mimics a law firm structure but caps fees (which they can do because of lower overhead, more efficient use of technology, and strategic employment of human capital), business customers can use an ALSP structured in this manner in almost any way they would use a law firm. An ALSP structured this way is also conducive to developing client relationships, unlike some of the other ALSP models explored in this section.

IN REAL LIFE

Frankie's Artistic Cement Pouring acquires one or two smaller cement pouring companies every year. Frankie hires a "full service" ALSP to handle the transactions. The ALSP connects Frankie with the appropriate lawyer on its staff to ensure the relationship runs smoothly, as would happen at a traditional law firm.

ALSPs to Support Corporate Legal Departments or Law Firms

These are ALSPs that may not be organized as law firms but provide assistance or "managed support" to corporate in-house legal departments or to law firms themselves. The insourced attorneys do any legal work through the legal department or law firm directly, which allows the ALSP to avoid the rules of professional conduct against the unauthorized practice of law.

The classification is a little gray, but that hasn't stopped some ALSPs from growing to thousands of lawyers operating in multiple jurisdictions.

Axiom, one of the earliest ALSPs, established in the year 2000, and Lawflex are examples of ALSPs that could provide this service.

IN REAL LIFE

Bernadette and Fred are business partners and co-founders of Super Awesome and Only Oatmeal Raisin Cookie Company. They disagree on whether their growing business needs a general counsel.

Bernadette and Fred compromise by obtaining a contract general counsel through an ALSP to dial in actual needs, clarify allocation of tasks, and establish lines of communication among the cookie company's leadership team. They agree to revisit a permanent general counsel role after this contract experiment has concluded.

ALSPs That Match Clients to Lawyers

Some ALSPs will evaluate a client's needs through a request for proposal or application and match each client to lawyers in their rosters with the appropriate expertise. These "matching services" don't typically regulate work or pricing and therefore equally can't monitor the relationship. An example of this type of ALSP is LegalShield, which operates via a membership model. Membership clients of LegalShield are matched with a law firm in their jurisdiction and from there matched with a lawyer with the right expertise to handle an inquiry. If the client needs more assistance, they can retain the lawyer on a further basis, at which point the relationship is between client and lawyer (and a traditional client-law firm relationship), and LegalShield is no longer involved.

IN REAL LIFE

Crystal is a sole proprietor who does welding out of her garage. She wonders if it is worth filing trademark applications on her welding designs. Crystal submits an application to an ALSP, which matches her to an intellectual property attorney.

ALSPs That Provide Precedent Agreements Customized to the Client's Specifications

This type of ALSP allows you to select the type of agreement you need.[45] Software leads you through a series of questions to allow customization, and for a relatively nominal fee, you can download the customized agreement. Rocket Lawyer is an example of this type of service.

IN REAL LIFE

Billy is the owner of Lots o' Guns + Stuff Shooting Range. His accountant advises him to establish a subsidiary. Billy downloads the corporate documentation from a popular ALSP that offers subsidiary documentation necessary to establish the Lots o' Guns + Stuff Retail Shop and the Lots o' Ammo + Stuff Annex.

ALSPs That Provide Specialized or Niche Services

Other ALSPs provide specific services such as document review or e-discovery and satisfy the needs of corporate in-house departments and law firms. As the industry has matured, many ALSPs have begun to offer more than one area of expertise.

---

45 This software as a service ("SaaS") category is not, in at least certain jurisdictions, considered an ALSP. Rather, SaaS companies are considered an exception to providing legal services which prevents them from being targeted for unauthorized practice of law. This distinction is less relevant to the client and more relevant to the operation and management of the service provider.

IN REAL LIFE

Jessica's Tree Trimmerz & Lawn Cleanup is embroiled in an ugly lawsuit after one of her employees caused several trees to fall on a client's home and garage. Jessica contacts her long-standing lawyer to discuss the need for cost-saving measures. Her lawyer recommends outsourcing discovery to an ALSP he's used in the past that can provide high-quality service and cost savings.

Mixed-Bag ALSPs

As the alternative legal market has matured, including through consolidation and mergers, many ALSPs have become mixed bags. For example, LegalZoom started off as a DIY legal document provider but later expanded its services to include lawyer support. Most ALSPs now offer a combination of the services listed above. Indeed, some of the providers I've mentioned are examples of more than one particular type of ALSP.

You can find more examples of how companies use ALSPs at manageyourlawyer.com/ALSP or scan the QR code below.

QUALITY CONTROL

Companies and law firms have reported quality concerns and the failure to save money as reasons they hesitate in using ALSPs. No doubt those concerns are valid.

But do those concerns differ from concerns with law firms? No law firm, no matter the size or reputation, can claim they have fully satisfied customers all the time.

The Big Four accounting firms[46] grew their share of the ALSP market to approximately $1.4 billion of a $13 billion industry at the end of 2019. That they are putting massive effort into continuing to grow that share is a good sign for a viable market. Indeed, law firms are establishing their own downstream ALSPs to compete with the external market. Whether law firms will succeed in their efforts remains to be seen, but it is at least another indication that ALSPs are here to stay.

In addition, legal regulatory bodies[47] interested in improving access to justice may open doors to permit ALSPs to grow unimpeded by regulatory concerns. For example, in August 2020, the Utah Supreme Court voted unanimously in favor of a two-year pilot program for alternative legal business models to provide innovative legal services more easily to Utah residents.

---

46 The Big Four accounting firms are Deloitte, Ernst & Young (EY), PricewaterhouseCoopers (PwC), and Klynveld Peat Marwick Goerdeler (KPMG).

47 "To Tackle the Unmet Legal Needs Crisis, Utah Supreme Court Unanimously Endorses a Pilot Program to Assess Changes to the Governance of the Practice of Law," Utah Courts, accessed May 19, 2022, https://www.utcourts.gov/utc/news/2020/08/13/to-tackle-the-unmet-legal-needs-crisis-utah-supreme-court-unanimously-endorses-a-pilot-program-to-assess-changes-to-the-governance-of-the-practice-of-law/.

There is great scope for ALSPs to serve any size of business, and any size of business can take advantage of the more favorable economic structures. These are all indications that ALSPs are becoming more mainstream and will continue to change the legal landscape in ways that will better satisfy customer demands.

SYSTEM SUGGESTIONS

As part of your process for retaining an attorney, be sure to consider whether an ALSP can do the work of a traditional law firm at more affordable rates. Do a little research and consult with trusted colleagues about their experiences with ALSPs the same way you vet traditional lawyers and law firms.

CHAPTER 10

REVIEWING YOUR
LEGAL BILL

You flip through your snail mail, reaching a fat envelope. The return address gives it away. It's your legal bill. There's an uncomfortable feeling in the pit of your stomach. You ignore that feeling and rip open the envelope. You casually flip through the pages, skimming the items for a "total amount," which you're still not seeing. You flip a few more pages as the furrow in your brow deepens.

Then you find it. The punch in the gut. The double line item. A curse passes your mouth and you toss the thing in your inbox for the light of another day.

Fee disputes are among the most common problems with lawyers. It's not hard to see why. Fees are high. Additional costs such as filing fees and other legal expenses are often misunderstood or unexpected. Clients are unhappy with the outcome or the lawyer's performance. Legal matters often drag out much longer than anticipated even when forewarned. And hello—law firms are still charging twenty-five cents a page for photocopying? Not many professions can get away with billing the way lawyers do.

Likely a highly understated issue is the usual and reasonable desire to avoid confrontation. If we don't find a problem, there won't be any problem to address. That position is enforced by the defeatist devil on your shoulder that says:

"It is what it is."

"What can I do about it anyway?"

"Why waste my time?"

"Fucking lawyers."

Those thoughts or derivations thereof develop in an instant, even semiconsciously, as that bill is tossed back into the physical or digital inbox. Depending on your circumstances, your expectation is that bothering to dive into it would only save you a few hundred, a few thousand, or even a few tens of thousands—where there simply isn't the right incentive to bother.

We all have a bandwidth and administrative tasks sometimes take a back seat to strategic decisions that your business relies on. But like all else in life, when we practice developing better habits, they become spontaneous. It's the very nature of a good or bad habit. Little effort is expended in accomplishing them. Like the green smoothie. Instead of a big morning production, it is an effortless behavior that makes you feel great. And when you don't have it, you miss it.

Just as with the green smoothie, reviewing your bill more effectively means you're playing your part in creating a more educated and powerful client. Even when we avoid some problems with a more robust courting process and better negotiated engagement letters, this process is still useful when it comes to legal bills.

This chapter sets out a process for reviewing your bill to find cost savings—on the lifesaving principle that money is better in your pocket than in your lawyer's. Also, you probably know this already, but lawyers play games in their *presentation* of the bill, and we'll talk about a few of those games so you're aware of them. Don't you need to know the rules to win the game?

STEP 1: BE TIMELY

Read your bill—which you should be receiving at least monthly—within twenty-four hours. Why twenty-four? Why not? It could be by end of business day or some other suitably identifiable and short time frame, but it sends the very powerful message to your brain that this is something you're responsible for, painful as a fulsome read may be. I know a lot of sophisticated business-people who do exactly as I described at the start of the chapter, including the furrow of the brow, the physiological pain in the gut, and the ensuing curse uttered from otherwise polite lips. If that's you, you're in good company.

It's time to change the behavior to replace casual disregard for careful reading. It's a prudent business move. Maybe you ultimately can't do anything about it. But maybe you can. And any businessperson should know generally where the money is going.

Timeliness in reviewing your bill also makes it easier to address problems as they arise. You will be less inclined to call your lawyer four months after receiving a bill that has a questionable research project or a meeting with counsel you've never heard of. You won't remember details the longer the bill sits, and the likelihood that you'll consider an overbilled amount as a sunk cost will climb.

STEP 2: PULL IT OUT
(YOUR ENGAGEMENT LETTER!)

Refresh your memory with the engagement letter so that you know what you agreed to, and simply reconcile those details to the bill. Note discrepancies to discuss with your lawyer.

Even if you agreed to something, that doesn't necessarily mean you are stuck with it. Many courts aren't swayed when a lawyer says, "But the client agreed to pay it in the engagement letter," if it turns out that fee otherwise isn't kosher. The engagement letter can't be used to justify unreasonable terms, including unreasonable fees. For example, if you agreed to pay certain overhead costs that are no longer permitted by the rules of professional conduct or fall in a gray area where guidance conflicts or goes unanswered, you may not be required to pay them.

But we're getting ahead of ourselves. For now, just consider whether there are things in the bill that you agreed to that are not consistent with the engagement letter or that are consistent with the engagement letter but that you find questionable.

STEP 3: READ WITH A CRITICAL MIND

Have the right questions in mind. Things like:

- Do you have enough details to ensure you can assess functions? If it's as you expected, you should be seeing appropriate dates and times as well as an adequate description of functions. For example, "agreement" and "research" without further explanation are, in many cases, shoddy bullshit that should be politely called out (other than as may be required to preserve confidentiality).

- Are there charges for nonlawyers like secretaries or other overhead?

- Are there too many people present at meetings or what appears to be insufficient delegation?

- Are there charges for discussing billing or other matters not strictly relating to your matter? (Most lawyers will not include details like this, but they might let them slip.)

- Are there duplicates or discrepancies for meetings you attended?

- Are there meetings that are not cross-referenced to your meeting log?

- Have there been undisclosed fee increases or outside lawyers hired?

- Are there charges for things like the Four Seasons?

- Is there any unethical behavior like discrepancies in the use of trust funds or your instructions—or outright lies (as far as you can tell)?

- Have undisclosed conflicts arisen or are billings made in ways you hadn't been told about?

- Has the lawyer adequately explained a certain function or what its purpose is and how it fits into your overall strategy?

- Do the tasks reflect what you've discussed or your instructions?

Have tough questions in mind. You'll be surprised by what is buried in the details.

STEP 4: BEWARE OF THE HUNGER GAMES

What business doesn't want to get paid? A lawyer can't be faulted for trying to draft a bill in a way that makes clients want to pay. Equally, clients should learn the tricks of the trade to protect themselves.

Basically, a lawyer will try to project a lot of effort, honesty, and fairness in a bill. Doing so makes a client feel like they are getting what they paid for. Your job is to better assess whether the effort *projected* is equivalent to the work *actually done*. And to make that assessment, you need to know how they try to increase projected effort (leaving aside actual effort).

Here are some basics (you'll find things like this in books written for lawyers and published by the ABA—in case you still believe the ABA is out for your best interests):

Paragraph Form Instead of Itemization

Many lawyers will give you a bill in paragraph form with a single fee at the end of that big, long paragraph rather than a line-by-line description of tasks with individual smaller fees. They do this because the paragraph form makes it feel like there's a lot of ongoing effort. And a whole bunch of smaller fees flashing before a client's eyes cheapens the value.

Except, if you are being billed by the hour, you should expect to see what goes into each one of those minutes. Request an itemization (and make it clear you expect you will not be billed for proper bill preparation).

Lots of Verbs

Consider "telephone call" versus "conference with opposing counsel to discuss deposition and negotiate terms."

Although the latter is what you'd like to see because it gives context to what was done, it also *conveys* more work and effort. Stringing one hundred items together gives a feeling of a lot of work. Maybe there was a lot of work done. But maybe there was just an overly high usage of verbs in the bill. To see through the fog, be aware of how a lot of verbs make you "feel."

Busy Pages

Seeing a big number on a page with lots of white space and little writing may look more elegant, but it gives the impression that not much was done for a big bill. As a result, many firms will put a lot of words on the page. And if there aren't that many words to say, they'll shrink the size of the paper. Yes, people do that.

STEP 5: ASK QUESTIONS!

Do you understand the entries? You're not going to know, nor should you expect to know, what absolutely everything means, but you should have a solid idea.

After a review, if you're concerned about your bill, consider, do you feel like you've been overbilled because of waste, incompetence, or bad ethics? Are you still confused about expenses?

A lawyer who cares about you as a client will not squirm at explaining entries and will address your concerns and correct mistakes. An even better lawyer will suggest cost-cutting techniques.

The upsides to this open dialogue are huge, especially compared to the downsides. Problems fester, and if you don't ask, you don't get. There are many diplomatic and productive ways to approach a billing dispute, and if nothing else, you've got a shot at getting a mutually agreeable reduction in your fees. That money can be spent in effective ways for your business and not your lawyer's. Plus, if you don't bring it up, you're just going to end up feeling worse about your lawyer, and suddenly you feel like a martyr, waiting for the next bill only to grow more frustrated.

NEGOTIATING POWER:
PUT YOUR CAPE ON

We've already covered negotiation generally in Chapter 5, but I want to reiterate a point about your negotiating *power*.

When it comes to billing, you have some negotiating power—and depending on how well you followed the other methods in the book, you may have more than you think. One reason a lawyer does not want a billing dispute with you is that they are usually reported to malpractice insurers (even where a dispute is settled in favor of the law firm).

Don't give in so easily if you really think your lawyer has been unreasonable or improper in their billing practices. As everywhere in life, be reasonable and as diplomatic as you can muster. That's not my specialty, but any of us can at least keep in mind the adage that you'll get more with honey.

THE TIME-VERSUS-MONEY CONUNDRUM

In the next chapter, we'll be covering how to find help for the dirty work: administrative work no one wants to do. For now, this chapter (and the ones leading up to it) are intended to at least shed light on the true costs so you can make smarter cost-benefit assessments. How you wish to carry out your responsibility in this regard is up to you, and only you can decide the tradeoff between time and money.

An article titled "How to Write a Good Invoice" on the ABA's website emphasizes the importance of billing clients and that it is "one of the most important tasks for lawyers" and that "bills say a lot about us."[48]

Agreed. Bills say a lot about lawyers. And it's time that the way *you* review your bills says something about you.

SYSTEM SUGGESTIONS

Upload your legal bills into your project management system in an appropriately labeled folder (for example, Invoices) under Month 1 (or other designated time frame). Create a checklist with the questions already reflected in this chapter and schedule time to review your bill promptly after receipt.

For examples relevant to these suggestions, scan the QR code below or visit manageyourlawyer.com/bills.

---

48   Teresa Beck, "How To Write a Good Invoice," American Bar Association, May 9, 2012, https://www.americanbar.org/groups/litigation/committees/woman-advo-cate/articles/2012/how-to-write-good-invoice/ behind the ABA's paywall.

CHAPTER 11

BECOME YOUR OWN DETECTIVE

It was early one Saturday evening in a savvy businesswoman's apartment, and we were surrounded by dozens of banker's boxes stuffed full of documents. She plopped an ice cube in my white wine, insisting that it was a perfectly acceptable way to chill it. She didn't like red. A tattered Pizza Hut box lay atop a nearby table littered with paper. We always ordered Pizza Hut pizza. She said it had the best crust.

Triple horrors.

It was the stage upon which this businesswoman managed to keep over $50,000 in her own pocket rather than her lawyer's. I was the cheap labor meant to cut down on legal costs—and cut down on legal costs we did.

A couple of years earlier, she'd started with a vision and pulled together several million dollars in financing, driving herself to pitch meetings and sleeping in her car to preserve funds for the new business. Unfortunately, the business was heavily dependent on new technology that had been promised but not delivered, ultimately resulting in the company's demise and a lawsuit against the service provider.

Wanting to keep legal fees under control, she spoke with her lawyer about outsourcing the document review and other aspects of the due diligence. That's where I was enlisted. I was a recent economics graduate and had no clue what document review was, but I was happy to make some extra money even if it meant working evenings and weekends, stopping for a few brief moments in each eighteen-plus-hour workday to eat cold pizza and drink warm wine. We were machines, working our way through boxes of documents on instruction from counsel.

Over the course of some weeks, I worked approximately 350 hours at $10 per hour. She worked alongside me when she could. Let's conservatively say that between the two of us, we took care of approximately 500 hours of work that otherwise would have been done largely by young associates and billed at a very conservative rate of $125 an hour.

$$500 \times \$10 = \$5,000$$

Compared to:

$$500 \times \$125 = \$62,500$$

This was a number of years ago, so if we adjust for inflation alone, that number would look more like $110,000. But if we adjust further for legal costs, which have trended upward 3–6 percent annually, much greater than the rate of inflation and much greater than the average cost of wage increases, we'd have to adjust for the fact that today's young associates are often billed out at much higher rates than $125 an hour. Even though it would also be hard to find the right person for $10 an hour, regular salaries have not increased with the same gusto as lawyer fees—meaning the cost savings in today's dollars would be significantly larger in scope.

Except...

It may be prudent for a big business with big legal bills to outsource certain functions in-house or externally. But the last thing a small business needs to add to an already stretched team's capacity is administrative work like document review, social media scrubs, finding documents through a malfunctioning government website, or some similar crap no one wants to do.

However, what if we had a better toolkit of research tips and tricks that we knew when and how to apply simply by asking the right questions like:

- What type of work can be appropriately outsourced?

- Can I do my own research?

- How will outsourcing affect the quality of the work?

- How do we find the right people to outsource to?

- How will outsourcing affect the relationship and level of cooperation with my lawyer?

This chapter will help you answer those questions and determine whether the time, expense, or risk of outsourcing will be worth it.

PRELIMINARY STEPS

No prudent business owner wants to pay more legal fees than they need to. Outsourcing can significantly cut down on those fees, so you'll want to ask at the start of your legal matter, as well as along the way as tasks become well defined, "Are there tasks that I or my team can take care of to reduce the financial burden?"

This question will be governed by three other considerations.

First, the availability of ALSPs (which we covered in Chapter 9) has made outsourcing easier. ALSPs are often the product of a greater desire to outsource. If you are working or plan to work with an ALSP, much of the information in this chapter will require only brief consideration. Chances are, your ALSP has already baked into its processes the outsourcing options considered here.

Second, if you worry that you'll embarrass yourself with outsourcing questions that are only for cheap barterers or that you'll be stepping on your lawyer's toes, don't. Big businesses and even law firms themselves have driven demand for ALSPs in large part to outsource tasks to specialists, to better use technology, and to control fees, all in the interest of keeping up with an evolving market to better address clients' needs.

There is nothing embarrassing about trying to spend your dollars more efficiently while improving the quality of the service you receive. Indeed, it's your obligation. Long gone should be the days when only large companies can take advantage of the changing legal landscape. Certainly, if big banks and investment firms take no issue with requesting accommodations and outsourcing, why should you? After the 2007–08 financial crisis, institutional clients were even less troubled by demanding fee stipulations and imposing billing requirements when hiring a law firm. Most big law firms complied to avoid losing their big business clientele.

Third, attorney-client privilege that protects communications between lawyers and clients (and client representatives) may be at significant risk when information is shared without appropriate precautions. It's important therefore that the implications of outsourcing be discussed and coordinated with your lawyer.

Outsourcing may not ultimately be appropriate, but it is something to be considered with what you learn in this chapter and aired out in an open and honest conversation with your attorney. If outsourcing doesn't make sense, then you don't need to pursue it—but develop the habit of making it part of your legal process.

Let's get to work to do that.

WHAT TYPE OF WORK CAN BE OUTSOURCED?

Outsourced work might include nonlegal and legal work. It includes legal and nonlegal research, regulatory risk and compliance services, litigation and investigative support, e-delivery services, contract management, intellectual property management, and other specialty legal services. Any number of tasks that do not require specialized expertise are also fair game.

That sounds like pretty much anything, and it is. From a practical perspective, it's easiest to think about in terms of work that forms a discrete chunk of your legal work, such as research, due diligence, or maintenance-type work, like the aforementioned regulatory work.

For example, your business may be the owner of several patents and trademarks. The administration and maintenance work could be outsourced to a service provider that specializes in IP maintenance, which could be much cheaper than a traditional law firm that does maintenance work as one of many service offerings. The specialty firm is likely to have more evolved and specific-use technology that makes its service offering more efficient and therefore less costly.

HOW DO I DO MY OWN RESEARCH?

Where information is in the public domain or is obtained through a simple internet search, you, a team member, a researcher, a virtual assistant, or a paralegal you hire as an

there are a lot of young, overpriced lawyers who equally know what they are doing and many senior lawyers who manage those younger lawyers (no serious person would le this reality). The key is to have solid instructions from lawyer or party managing the process on the one hand, and ious and capable people—lawyers or nonlawyers—on the her.

the example I provided, I received clear instructions from oth my colleague and her lawyer, along with fair supervision nd open lines of communication, which ultimately preserved he quality of the work.

In general, the quality of outsourced work can be encouraged or preserved from appropriate delegation to people qualified to do the work, clear instructions, adequate supervision, and a firm grasp of how the outsourced work fits into the larger project. It's not the designation of "lawyer" that dictates the execution of those practices.

HOW DO WE FIND THE RIGHT PEOPLE AND PLACES TO OUTSOURCE TO?

My old boss was smart in asking me to help her. Not because I was a broke recent graduate but because she already had some experience with my work and could trust that I would be able to follow directions the way she and her lawyer needed me to. As you would any other outsourcing decision in business, use the processes you already have developed within your business, including referrals, interviews, and reviews, to find the right people.

independent contractor can take care of work just as easily as a high-priced lawyer or staff member at a law firm. Consider further that your knowledge of your business and your industry, almost assuredly better than your lawyer's, may make you, your team, or even someone you hire better suited to the job.

Part of what scares people about research is that they don't know where to start. Below are a few guidelines to remove some of that uncertainty, and you'll find plenty more detail and resources by scanning the QR code below or heading to manageyourlawyer.com/resources.

- Many vital records,[49] like birth, death, marriage, and divorce certificates, are available to the public in different places depending on the state.

- There's a difference between public records and publicly available information. Public records refer to information that is not confidential

---

49 The National Vital Statistics System is here: https://www.cdc.gov/nchs/nvss/index.htm.

You may get information on where to write for vital records in all states here: "Where to Write for Vital Records," Centers for Disease Control and Prevention, January 25, 2019. https://www.cdc.gov/nchs/w2w/index.htm?CDC_AA_refVal=https%3A%2F%2Fwww.cdc.gov%2Fnchs%2Fw2w.htm.

and generally pertains to government conduct, whereas publicly available information is found in the public sphere, like on a website or in a newspaper. An example of a public record is a certificate of incorporation that you may want to see for a potential business partner to verify its proper existence. Public records tend to contain information more difficult to find because it's not always apparent where to look for it, especially when maneuvering through outdated or inefficient government websites and portals. There may also be a cost to access them.

- Social media is a treasure trove of information relating to a person's personal or professional history, whereabouts, contacts, and so on.

- There are a lot of tricks to everyday internet searches.[50] DuckDuckGo, Opera, Google, or any other search engine are more powerful than the average user understands.

- Sunshine laws, like the Freedom of Information Act and Privacy Act and similar state statutes, were enacted to provide transparency and disclosure of government information. Anyone can make applications under these statutes, and they could be useful in many circumstances. For example, a real

---

50   Carole A. Levitt and Mark E. Rosch, *The Cybersleuth's Guide to the Internet* (Internet For Lawyers Inc., 2019).

estate developer struggling to fin
with a commissioner's office on a
may be interested in filing a sunshi
for closed-door meetings.

- Many public libraries host expensive
services and access to databases that y
access to with a free library card. These
could be used to find information about a
or company you are about to deal with in
for example.

Like in many areas of life, some skills take a litt
master, but the dividends can be huge and long-lasti

HOW WILL OUTSOURCING AFFECT TH QUALITY OF THE WORK?

In the example I gave at the start of the chapter, you might
wondered what a newly graduated student who hadn't yet g
to law school knew about document review. It's a fair que
tion. I learned only in conversations from my colleague tha
document review or "due diligence" was simply the process o
reviewing documents for sensitive or bolstering information
to enhance each side's case. It is often the most labor-intensive
(and costly) stage of litigation.

No cost savings is worth potentially missing key details in your
documents. So was it prudent to leave it to "nonexperts" to
identify potentially case-saving material?

Beyond that, here are some ideas on where to outsource:

- Delegate tasks to an employee, a virtual assistant, a serious student, or your kid who is looking for some work, has talents that match the task at hand, and is willing to take good and clear instruction. Furthermore, the work that you or your team does can always provide a good starting point from which your lawyer can provide further verification.

- Freelance sites like Upwork or Freelancer have hundreds of providers for document or due diligence review by lawyers, paralegals, or virtual assistants of different experience levels, accompanied by an extensive network of user reviews.

- Certain law firms provide "unbundled" legal services, which simply could be described as à la carte legal services (or "discrete" legal processes, as mentioned earlier).

- Your law firm could coordinate an outsourcing option. As mentioned previously, law firms are big users of ALSPs.

- Artificial intelligence is creating outsourcing options for a broader array of clients. Legal technology is constantly available and, depending on the size of your business, could be a suitable option.

Appropriate delegation may save you thousands. Consider the role of delegation in your business and extrapolate use to your legal matter.

HOW WILL OUTSOURCING AFFECT THE RELATIONSHIP AND LEVEL OF COOPERATION WITH MY LAWYER?

Generally speaking, lawyers secure in their skin will not take issue with outsourcing. Others might.

Like a good therapist or better self-care, the ever-changing business and legal landscape will help alleviate these insecurities. First, as outsourcing continues to become more common, there will be fewer issues. Second, it's worth noting where legal insecurities are most prevalent. It's not the grade A law firms that need to worry about a changing legal landscape. Even if they mature and grow and merge, they will likely remain the first choice for the world's largest corporations, and there's no reason to expect those firms will not continue to thrive.

Not so for lower tiers of legal service. Think of it as the grades of sushi restaurants. There's the top sushi—the grade A firms— and then there are varying levels of sushi below that. They serve their purpose to satisfy a quick sushi craving, but they're always at greater risk of going out of business. True, even grade A can go out of business—and they do. But even if a grade A sushi restaurant closes shop, the chef will reopen somewhere else. Those middle and lower tiers are far more insecure. And that insecurity is more likely to be the source of friction.

Have an open and honest conversation with your lawyer about suitable places for outsourcing. There may be none, or your lawyer may explain clearly why outsourcing could cost you rather than save you money or destroy attorney-client privilege. You should get a sense from this conversation as to whether there will be friction that will interfere with outsourcing efforts. If it starts smelling fishy, you should consider a more proactive approach to identify the outsourcing options available. Or consider a lawyer with a more evolved view of the legal industry.

At this point, you've got most of the details you need to carry out a kick-ass relationship with your lawyer. But in the next chapter, let's turn to starting that relationship off on the right foot.

SYSTEM SUGGESTIONS

In the course of your early discussions with your lawyer and as timelines and workflows start to take shape, schedule a meeting with your lawyer to discuss possible outsourcing options in light of safeguards to preserve privilege.

CHAPTER 12

YOU'RE HIRED!

EVEN FOR RELATIONSHIPS NOT INVOLVING SEX, THERE'S still a surge of excitement. Starting off with a handshake is fun, and no matter how guarded the relationship, that human contact creates a bond that opens a relationship to new and wonderful things.

Which is why the awkward elbow bump is not going to stick long term, as much as I adore change. (Keep your hands clean and don't touch your face!)

Unfortunately, the excitement often dies unless there's something to keep it going. A trusting and sincere relationship is a good thing to keep it going, and if we can have that by finding the right person in the first place, all the better.

We'll discuss some dos and don'ts to finding your lawyer since we're almost to the end of the book and we've not had a dos and don'ts list yet. We'll assemble all these details in a single card in the Trello board to keep you organized and thinking straight.

When you are next considering hiring a lawyer, you need only do a quick scan of the list and think about what questions are most relevant to the hiring decision. Doing appropriate due diligence at this stage will keep things hot and spicy.

DOS

Do Fully Consider whether You Need a Lawyer at All

A few questions directed to trusted friends or advisors may be all that is necessary to think through the most basic of preliminary questions: do you even need a lawyer? Your existing network can be super helpful here, even if you have to maneuver the confidentiality jungle. People are almost always willing to help when you give them a reason.

Do Define Your Legal Issue

What do you need accomplished, and what is your end result? Be crystal clear so you can explain your needs to a prospective lawyer.

Do Ask Your Network

After the first two easy dos, this is the most important. Ask people in your network if they have firsthand experience with a lawyer dealing with a similar problem you now face. Notice this is much more specific than just a lawyer referral. Specifically, seek a lawyer who has a proven track record with someone you trust. Be creative in how you preserve confidential information, but be clear in what you need and are looking for. People are quick to give a recommendation for a lawyer they like or know. You're after much more than that, and a lawyer that a friend or trusted colleague just likes or knows is almost as worthless as likes on a social media post.

Do Consider the Multitude of Services Offered outside a Traditional Law Firm

Thinking back to Chapter 9 on ALSPs, can you use a less traditional model? Of course, you want to ensure quality and confidentiality are not sacrificed in favor of a lower cost, so the remaining points of due diligence still matter.

Do Ask a Lawyer You Already Trust

Perhaps you've worked with Gandalf on a corporate law matter, and now you need a trust and estates lawyer. If you've been happy with Gandalf, you can ask for a recommendation for someone they have firsthand experience with. Just remember that just because you like your lawyer doesn't mean you'll like their recommendation, and lawyers are often too quick to recommend someone they went to school with or met at a networking event hoping the favor comes back to them. Be frank, and ask Gandalf to be frank.

Do Ask the Right Questions but Not All Questions

Rather than focus on a generic list of questions, which a lot of freebie articles online will give you, really think about what you need to know to make a wise hiring decision. Does the lawyer have experience with your type of problem? If it's a litigation matter, how many cases have they won? If it's an intellectual property matter, is the lawyer qualified and registered by the Patent and Trademark Office? Or do they dabble? Consider what's truly important.

Do Financial Due Diligence

Include questions that go directly to billing, such as a breakdown of costs for various stages of the legal matter you face. That way, you can make a better cost-benefit analysis. Or consider an ALSP or any number of other decisions that stem from a better understanding of expected costs.

Do Put a Detective Hat On

Unfortunately, it's very difficult to find out the real dirt on someone, but there are a few ways to do a background check. You can start with your lawyer prospect's disciplinary history. Some bar associations have this information available online or you may need to phone them. To check these details, go to the state's bar association website and look for a tab that says something like "For the public." However, the fact that a lawyer is in good standing isn't enough. Consider the research you'd do for a legal adversary: a good solid internet search to see if they've been featured in any news, as well as case information sites available in your state. As with many other areas, you'll also want to consider other lawyers' opinions because they may have inside information on reputation.

Do Sit Face-to-Face or, at a Minimum, on an Online Call

You're human. You've got instincts. What's their body language saying? If you're visiting in person, can you get a sense of how they "live"? Are there a bunch of miserable people around? What else do your business antennae tell you about this person?

DON'TS

Don't Rely on Ratings

Let's say a couple approaches a lawyer for an amicable divorce, and the lawyer explains conflicts and is ultimately hired by the wife for whom the lawyer does a terrible job, including failing to file documents in a timely fashion. The husband leaves her a bad Google review. The lawyer, who was apparently a hop, skip, and tiniest of leaps away from retirement, sues the husband. To dispose of the matter, the husband settles with the lawyer for a small sum and removal of the review to allow her to fly off into the white-jacketed sunset. It wouldn't be the first time a lawyer sued someone over a bad Google review.

Such is the trust level that should be granted to online ratings. In addition to adequate sample size, which is rarely the case, people most likely to write reviews are those on the extremes due to a really great experience or a particularly bad one. What good professional hasn't had both? Furthermore, just because a client doesn't like their result doesn't mean the lawyer did a bad job (then again, that may be fair enough—trying doesn't cut it, but results do). Although the public's reviews of things like a hotel or restaurant can offer good feedback, it's a much tougher exercise in the legal arena.

But a Google review is not as sophisticated as a legal review, such as Chambers—or is it? Ask any lawyer, and chances are they can point to someone on one of "those lists" they know would never on planet Earth make the cut. But they do in a Chambers or Martindale ranking.

They're often dubious, "sophisticated" in name only, and could rely on unsophisticated methodologies. Stars, letters, points? No matter. It's often lawyers picking their friends or colleagues that feed these algorithms, not all that much better than the scratch-the-back type of "endorsements" you see on LinkedIn.

Don't Rely on Referrals

"Referral" doesn't just mean "someone you know" or "someone you know who knows someone." It *could* be someone you know, but only if all the other elements of your due diligence are satisfied.[51] The referral should be considered nothing more than a lead. A referral from someone who had a simple will drawn up when you have a complicated tax and estates matter to deal with may or may not help.

IN REAL LIFE

Maverick asked his friend Kenzo, a highly respected criminal lawyer (I know, I know) for a divorce lawyer recommendation. Kenzo recommended a highly regarded boutique family law firm, so Maverick called to meet with their attorneys.

They were awful. Like sometimes lawyers joke about the A team and B team, but the attorneys from the law firm were the D team from top to bottom, despite their fancy status. It mattered nothing that they enjoyed a reputation among lawyers. And that's the problem. The voice of clients is so quiet, it is but a whisper—like the quiet talker on that *Seinfeld* episode that resulted in Jerry looking like the Count of Monte Cristo. But she sure found her voice at the end.

Maverick ultimately fired the firm and hired another to get back on track, but not after tens of thousands of dollars were wasted.

---

51 Clio's Legal Trends Report 2019 found that 59 percent of its sample of 2,000 clients sought a referral when looking for a lawyer. Fifty-seven percent said they do their own research to find a lawyer, and only 16 percent reported doing both. Interestingly, 18 percent said they would never seek a referral from a friend or family member. The report can be downloaded by visiting https://www.clio.com/resources/legal-trends/2019-report/.

The Moral

Your referral is a lead, not a judgment. That lead may become judgment, but only after all other elements of your due diligence have been satisfied.

Don't Assume There Will Be Any Kumbaya Moments

You are looking for a trusted advisor. That is not the same thing as a friend. Consider how you feel when you are trying to advise a customer or client, but they just want to hear what they want to hear. It feels weird, and worse, it prevents you from serving them in the best way. No good lawyer will present themselves as a friend, nor should you seek that type of advisor (which is not to say that friendships cannot eventually develop).

Don't Take a Bulldog for the Sake of the Bulldog

As a corporate lawyer, I was taught to live by the principle that we should never tell a client something couldn't be done; rather, we should find a way to make a deal happen. In the complex but oft-flexible corporate world, that was a good rule of thumb. But when it comes to other areas of law, such as litigation, it doesn't do a client any good to hear from their litigator that you should "Fight! Fight! Fight!"

Sure, you can always fight...until your last dollar. The bulldog personality can be great! Especially compared to lawyers who lose some of that fight in favor of diplomacy that often *doesn't* ultimately serve the client or the legal profession. Lawyers exist in a dichotomous environment where on the one hand they are vivid competitors fighting for their clients, and on the other, they are equally incentivized to support metaphysical incestuous relationships and hesitate before calling out bad behavior. Although everyone makes mistakes and allowances should obviously be made for errors in the normal course, the bar at which lies, misrepresentations, and unethical behavior are called out by law firms, judges, and regulatory bodies appears to be way too high. And it leaves clients at a serious disadvantage.

IN REAL LIFE

A homicide investigator collected compelling evidence against Kyle, who was accused of raping a juvenile. Kyle's attorney, Ephraim O'Treetop, insisted Kyle was innocent. Kyle's grandma believed it, despite images and other evidence to the contrary, and funded Kyle's legal defense. Granny Kyla, undeterred from cleaning out her savings to save her "innocent grandson," also pledged the family's land in payment of legal fees. With the prosecutor willing to proceed to trial and undeterred by Ephraim's attempts to delay trial, Ephraim suggested it might be wise for Kyle to take a plea agreement. Kyle pled guilty and took the fifteen to twenty years the prosecutor offered—the same deal he had been offered months previously, before Granny Kyla's funds had been depleted and the land assigned for payment to defense counsel.

Kyle was lucky that the prosecutor stuck to the original plea offer. Sometimes prosecutors aren't so happy about having to work for months on a deal after attempting to be fair, and he might have added another five or ten years to the plea arrangement, making Kyle worse off than if Ephraim had not advocated fighting.

The Moral

As many experienced law enforcement officers say, "You're innocent until you're broke."

Sadly, there are lawyers who will push a case when their client could have reached a favorable deal $50,000 ago. Ultimately, you want a bulldog that knows when to turn on the pussy cat. That requires staying abreast of the particularities of your case, as covered in the rest of this book.

Don't Make a Decision Based on Cost Alone

Like a good bottle of wine, cost can give you an idea of quality, but it sure doesn't define it. Unlike wine, when you get too cheap, you need to be extra careful. Is a lawyer discounting fees to compete on price all that different than a heart surgeon offering a two-for-one sale? It's not likely to be the lawyer (or heart surgeon) you want. A lawyer charging less because of less experience may not be cheaper when you get the final bill, but they could be. Without considering other factors, it's impossible to say based on cost alone.

By now, it should be obvious that adequate due diligence depends on the totality of your evidence and not just any one "do" or "don't" rule. Still, this "don't" bears its own heading because far too many people are driven only by the hourly cost of the lawyer. Also, by now it should be clear that there is far more than just hourly cost that goes into the total cost assessment.

Don't Think You're So Special

Far be it from me or anyone else to stifle your individuality. Everyone is special. But in the words of Mark Manson[52] and in the spirit of not deluding ourselves, "if everyone were extraordinary, then by definition no one would be extraordinary."

Indeed. I know your legal matter feels horribly personal and private and unique to you, but the good thing is that, while totally unique (especially since every lawyer likes to claim they don't do commodity work and only do the special-est of the special to make sure you feel special—and that all that specialness necessitates big fees), chances are there's at least a big chunk of your legal matter that is not so special. What that means for you, in finding the right lawyer, is asking the right questions with respect to expertise, experience, and results. If your lawyer claims to have "lots of experience with your matter," then ask for details because they should be very willing and able to provide them.

---

52 Mark Manson, *The Subtle Art of Not Giving a F*ck: A Counterintuitive Approach to Living a Good Life* (New York: HarperOne, 2016).

See also "In Defense of Being Average," Mark Manson, accessed May 19, 2022, https://markmanson.net/being-average.

It seems like a lot, but all this comes down to is a well-articulated list of questions and implementing a very simple and straightforward system to ensure you do what you need to.

That will bring you much further down the road to having to utter the words you don't want to have to utter because you're not hosting *The Apprentice*.

SYSTEM SUGGESTIONS

Assemble these details in a single folder labeled The Hiring Decision, which will fall under the section of your project management tool called Before I Hire My Lawyer. When next considering a hiring decision, consider the items on the list, and proceed from there to complete your due diligence.

CHAPTER 13

YOU'RE FIRED!

ISN'T THERE A FAMOUS LINE ABOUT NOT KNOWING WHAT you don't know?

How does a nonlawyer know if their lawyer has acted outside the bounds of "reasonably competent" or otherwise made a mistake rising to the level of being fired? If we accept that lawyers are just people who put their pants on the same way, it's probably very reasonable that they make some mistakes, just like the rest of us. How many, though, and which ones are big enough to warrant losing their job as your counsel? If they charge you big fees, shouldn't they or their insurers pay for some mistakes rather than you? And what if those costs include unrecoverable ones, especially consequences of mistakes, like losing your legal case or the stress the mistakes cause?

We learn young that no superhero with latex skin is coming to save us. Similarly, when you run into problems where you feel your lawyer isn't right for you anymore, the only one who will save you is *you*. This highly unsatisfactory answer—which is unfortunately the answer we get for most of life's problems—does have guidelines that can be put to good strategic use.

This chapter will address some of those guidelines and considerations before you give your lawyer a pink slip.

REASONS TO FIRE

The decision to fire your lawyer is kind of like deciding to quit your job. You have to seriously consider whether the grass will be greener on the other side of the fence.

Lots of articles online will advise you on the considerations for firing a lawyer, but—like much of the information available to the public regarding advice on lawyers—it mostly falls in the basket of generic principles. Principles that don't have much basis in business reality or don't help people get to a yes or no answer. Where's the honest perspective of the businessperson who's in it for the survival of their business and life? I don't mean to get all dramatic, but these articles scattered all over the internet aren't empowering and aren't saving anyone money.

But sure, let's at least begin with a few basic questions that set aside our emotional selves. (It's wrong for a spicy Mediterranean-blooded woman to lead you through this exercise, but it's my obligation as the author.)

So why are you thinking about firing your lawyer? Maybe it's one of these reasons:

- You don't like a court ruling or the applicable law.

- You want things to move faster.

- You don't like a particular characteristic of your lawyer.

By themselves, these aren't likely good reasons to fire your lawyer. On the other hand, maybe you're thinking of firing the leech because:

- Your lawyer doesn't follow instructions.

- You're constantly confused about the law or legal process pertaining to your issue *despite* having asked for clearer explanations.

- You've been misled or misinformed about the legal process as it pertains to your matter or about the results this lawyer can achieve for you.

- Communications are horrible and prevent you from working as a team, including waiting days for a response or hearing excuses about late documents.

- This lawyer needs to be reminded about too many facts relevant to your case, forgets or changes meetings, misses court or other important business deadlines, makes duplicate requests for documents or other information you've already provided, and demonstrates similar sophomoric behavior.

In that case, maybe it's time to weigh the risks of firing your lawyer—namely, delay in your case moving forward and the additional cost to get someone else up to speed.

Once you've determined that you have a valid reason to fire your lawyer, then you can do a next-level assessment.

FIRING ASSESSMENT

There are lots of good reasons to end a professional relationship. There are also some good ones to avoid it. Let's consider the following to make sure we are making a wise decision.

Second Chances

Can you talk to them? It often helps even the most strained relationships. There may be misunderstandings that can be overcome, including by looking at some of your own communication shortcomings and better letting your lawyer know what you need. Taking an honest look back at where the relationship may be going wrong isn't an easy thing to do, especially for a relationship that doesn't seem overly important in life, like with your lawyer. But if a conversation with your lawyer can help, it's worth a shot.

Follow up any such conversation with a memo, something like, "Thank you for talking and for allowing me to be frank. Just to recap our meeting..." and complete the thoughts. Most lawyers want you to be happy because the happier you are, the more you continue to pay your bills. And reputational damage is, in many cases, a strong motivator. Many lawyers will honestly reflect on how they can make you happier, so give them a chance. At least one.

Like Just Right

You don't necessarily need to like your lawyer but even if their practice is good, if they suck to deal with, they're not going to be that good *for you*. Similarly, if they rarely perform for you and you keep losing when you should be winning, they're not going to be that good for you either, no matter how much you enjoy having closing drinks together. After those obvious thresholds and with fair expectations in seeking a business advisor and not a friend, consider whether there is enough of the right combination of performance and likability.

Timing

If you're approaching a critical point in your legal matter—like the signing of a term sheet or other important agreement, or an upcoming motion or other court appearance, or a critical negotiation of some sort—firing your lawyer at that point may not be the right thing to do. That could put your matter at a serious disadvantage. If you aren't sure whether there is an appropriate break in the proceeding or your deal, use whatever business acumen you have in conjunction with advice from another lawyer you're considering hiring. A more suitable lawyer will be happy to help you spearhead the best path forward.

Is Someone Waiting in the Wings?

Who's going to take your lawyer's place? If you had to fire an employee, in all likelihood you'd have someone lined up and ready to take the place of the person just canned. In case there was any doubt, that necessitates repeating the entire due diligence process covered in previous chapters. However cringe-worthy, a second lawyer competent to assist can at least guide your decision making to supplement your business judgment after considering all the factors in this list.

Review Your Engagement Letter

Once you're ready to move forward, check your engagement letter which is likely to set out some process requirements before you can move on. At least in civil matters, clients are most often fully entitled to fire their lawyers at will. Even if most jurisdictions in the United States don't permit a lawyer to withhold files for nonpayment of bills, as a practical matter, you'll get more cooperation when bills are paid. Your engagement letter is worth a quick reference to ensure you understand the process your lawyer foresees in the event you've given them the boot.

Have Your New Lawyer Do the Dirty Work

Generally, advice to cower from your obligations is piss-poor. Here? Up to you how you feel about it, but if you honestly feel like your lawyer hasn't done right by you while you've been paying them absurd dollars or even reasonable dollars and have had to go through the effort of finding another lawyer and the stress and expense of all of that, fuck it—get your new lawyer to send the letter to the old counsel that they are off the case and to send you files and do what they're supposed to do. If your original lawyer won't release files until bills are paid, your new lawyer will be able to provide advice on how best to maneuver this. That said, I have seen new lawyers acquiesce too quickly to this demand. In that case, remind them that lawyers cannot generally hold documents hostage despite bills being paid up or not. Once that bill is paid, any fee dispute that follows pertaining to that work is unlikely to be productive.

The Real Dirty Work

I have a good friend who entered the business world instead of the legal profession shortly after our graduation from law and business and is a master at managing people. He's the kind of guy who fires someone and ends up with them apologizing and asking my friend—the one who just fired them—out for a beer. No hard feelings. Brilliant.

Legal matters can be very emotional, even those we don't expect to be so emotional, like business deals. (Like, is that not the understatement of the year?) Whether you're concerned with the feelings of the person you're firing or not, there's usually some benefit to tact. If you're worried about not keeping your cool, definitely follow the advice in the aforementioned point and outsource the task.

Speaking with a seasoned colleague can help this process tremendously, to state the obvious, and of course, there's always just taking your ball and going home, too. The decision to drop a legal matter is a big deal, but it's all the more reason you need good counsel to help you navigate that decision making. Admittedly, it's unsatisfactory to decide between dropping the whole thing and praying for the best and using your best judgment as you would in any other business case. But it does at least reemphasize the point that the due diligence you exercise with your hiring decision is even more important.

THE CLUB

A client may still choose to sue their attorney for malpractice, and a sanction by a bar association (as discussed in Chapter 7) is likely to bolster the client's case. But even then, there are challenges:

- Finding a good lawyer willing to sue another. Despite the number of lawyers willing to take your money, that may not be the easiest task in the world depending on your community.

- Funding the expense of what would surely be a costly litigation.

- Facing the inability to recover because the lawyer may not have the assets with which to pay.[53]

---

53 Some states do not require lawyers to have professional liability insurance which makes recovery even more difficult.

- Coping with the stress of managing a litigation, knowing that the person you hired and paid to help you has screwed you.

- Suing someone may feel good for five minutes, but it doesn't always get you the closure or relief you really need.

It's no wonder many will forgo the life-sucking experience of having to sue their lawyer—the person they had hoped would be their biggest advocate. As we mentioned before when we discussed billing, win or lose, lawyers must report claims to their malpractice insurers, so there could be scope to threaten a suit, which may or may not be successful.

This chapter is not intended to depress you. It's intended to remind you that there are lots of good reasons for reading this book—well done! As they say, relationships last for different seasons. Sometimes the season ends and you need to move on for your business's sake, for your own sake, or both.

SYSTEM SUGGESTIONS

Assemble these details in a single folder labeled The Firing Decision, which will fall under the section of your project management tool called Ongoing. When next considering a firing decision, review the items on the list, and proceed from there to complete your due diligence.

CONCLUSION

BEFORE THE LAW

"Before the Law stands a doorkeeper. To this doorkeeper there comes a man from the country and prays for admittance to the Law..."

SO BEGINS A PARABLE WRITTEN IN 1914 BY BOHEMIAN author Frank Kafka.[54] It is a good reminder that humans have always been human, and—however one may interpret the wide-open quality of Kafka's writings—the law has been and will likely remain wrought with challenges that defy its inherent nature.

The rest of the parable goes like this. The man at the door is trying to get into the Law, thinking it should be accessible to everyone at any time. The doorkeeper says he can't grant admittance at the moment, so the man asks if he can get in later. "It

---

54 Translation by Ian Johnston: Franz Kafka, "Before the Law," Franz Kafka Online, accessed May 19, 2022, https://www.kafka-online.info/before-the-law.html.

is possible," he is told. Since the door is open, the man pokes his head inside only to be told by the laughing doorkeeper, "If you are so drawn to it, just try to go in despite my veto. But take note: I am powerful. And I am only the least of the doorkeepers. From hall to hall, there is one doorkeeper after another, each more powerful than the last."

The man decides to wait for permission. On a stool he sits "for days and years," trying to negotiate, bargain, and bribe his entry until all of his worldly possessions are gone and he sits a grumbly old man, still fixated on this single obstacle embodied in this doorkeeper. His eyesight begins to fail, and he curses his bad luck. And then the parable ends with this paragraph:

> Yet in his darkness he is now aware of a radiance that streams inextinguishably from the gateway of the Law. Now he has not very long to live. Before he dies, all his experiences in these long years gather themselves in his head to one point, a question he has not yet asked the doorkeeper. He waves him nearer, since he can no longer raise his stiffening body. The doorkeeper has to bend low towards him, for the difference in height between them has altered much to the man's disadvantage. "What do you want to know now?" asks the doorkeeper; "you are insatiable." "Everyone strives to reach the Law," says the man, "so how does it happen that for all these many years no one but myself has ever begged for admittance?" The doorkeeper recognizes that the man has reached his end, and to let his failing senses catch the words roars in his ear: "No one else could ever be admitted here, since this gate was made only for you. I am now going to shut it."

This brilliant parable has evoked theories and interpretations till the moos come home. At its heart, arguably, is that the law was not accessible to everyone when Kafka wrote *Before the Law* in 1914.

It isn't today either.

That the law is inaccessible is easy to believe. Except—fascinatingly—people believe it for vastly different and often conflicting reasons.

Defense counsel sitting in a courtroom defending a twenty-time serial offender with "Resist!" stickers on his laptop argues that the legal system is inaccessible and society at large is to blame for the plight of his client.

A young woman, doubtful that she will ever find justice for the trauma she now must live with for the rest of her life, appears in court to make a victim statement against her rapist who now seeks leniency.

A small businessman wonders whether there is any point to wading through contradictory laws and stifling rules to persevere through one challenging business problem after another to grow and scale a business, or if he should throw in the towel, stop innovating, and get a "regular" job for the security of a paycheck.

If the law, haphazardly applied at best and corruptly and maliciously applied at worst, isn't the clearest indication we live within a screen airing a Monty Python movie, I'm not sure what is. *Before the Law* explains that reality in whatever way you want it to, based on how you see the world.

Remembering that we don't need permission from a door-keeper or anyone else to walk into the law and take advantage of its halls requires:

- A proactive lion rather than a reactive sheep.

- Getting past the urge to be lazy and leaving to your lawyer the things you can or should do for yourself but don't want to because they're too hard or uncomfortable.

- Understanding that having a confidant and trusted advisor in your lawyer demands better use of your business and personal skills to create that dynamic; it's a two-way street.

- Knowing we can always become more of that which we seek by improving whatever natural tendencies or shortcomings negatively affect our relationship with our lawyer.

This book provides a system to better approach your lawyer and your legal matters to help save you money and a lot of stress using skills you have already developed in your business (and personal) life. For reasons we've touched on, those skills are not often put to good enough use when it comes to dealing with a lawyer.

It's time to stop. It's time to give yourself the gift of ownership and control. It doesn't mean it will be easier. It means you're a leader. And you're not a quitter.

Even applying one single strategy at a time could do wonders for your legal results and beyond. Consider that a single communication technique could change the course of conversations for the rest of your life—including with your lawyer—and ultimately prevent miscommunication, duplication of effort, and a larger bill. Consider that a more proactive attitude with your lawyer will ensure you also ask your doctor or accountant the right questions that protect your life and that of your business. Consider that simply acknowledging your own negotiating power gives you the opportunity to ask, and receive, a 10 percent reduction in fees and is enough to make that next deal happen.

I hope you'll be encouraged to use the framework presented here to draw and build on the amazing skills you already have. One of the greatest disservices we do to ourselves is to compare our talents to others to the point that we diminish the skills with which we are bestowed. Each one of us has an incredible gift of contribution and service using exactly what we have at our disposal at any given time. The only failure is in holding on to our egomaniacal arrogance that we have no more to learn. That the "easy stuff" doesn't warrant deep work or discussion in the way the quantitative or hard analyses do.

Go forth, and don't let a lawyer or the legal system crush your entrepreneurial spirit. Don't let a powerless doorkeeper convince you that you don't have some measure of control as you cross the threshold, before the law and through the halls of justice.

That access is yours for the taking, leaving the victim persona behind to better manage the relationship with your legal advisors.

To do otherwise would be a disservice to the business gods. And to you.

ACKNOWLEDGMENTS

I'VE NEVER WRITTEN ONE OF THESE SO BEAR WITH ME.

I know everyone says writing a book is hard. And it is. But honestly, it made me see how many people are out there to help you. Naturally, there are always people to help you if you pay them. But even if you don't pull out your credit card or crypto wallet, it's amazing what people will do for no return whatsoever. For their invaluable comments and feedback, I thank:

Scott L. Semer, an otherworldly creative talent, tax lawyer, screenwriter, filmmaker, and brilliant eccentric I've had the pleasure of working with and knowing since my lawyering days; Len Liscio, the best brother in the world who appreciates that all my questions, tech-related or otherwise, are of an urgent nature (and still, he takes all my calls); Vitania Liscio, my incredibly funny and witty cousin whose keen insights keep insane times sane and whose sales and design skills keep the world spinning beautifully; Christine Fisher, whose ever-sharp intellect pierces through her piercing eyes to see everything—she's the most dependable confidante a girl could've met early in law school; Richard Nolan, whose willingness to speak unconventionally about business defines his talent for unfucking fucked-up companies, and has kept me laughing since business school days drinking beer out of rugby boots (and did you really drink all those fish at that weird party? It's rather hazy...); Jason Moyse, for getting his hands dirty to brave the world of law firm technology and management as so few do; Michael E. Young, lawyer and entrepreneur, who seems to enjoy pushing outside the bubble as much as I do; and Dale Linton—one of the hot ex-boyfriends referenced in the book because hot exes are meant to be enjoyed as long as possible—whose ever-positive vibes, easy laughs, and thoughtful reflections are a joy.

You are all super cool and I know "thank you" isn't enough. (Apologies also: the failures to fully absorb your excellent comments resulting in any shortcomings in this book are the fault of shortcomings in my brain...I'm working on fixing those but there's only so much God gave me to work with and I'm doing my best.)

To my incredible friend and colleague, Beverly Behan, one of the world's foremost corporate governance experts, for staring me in the eye and saying, "That's your first book," and her encouragement to just write the damn thing. Bev, you're a constant source of inspiration and always know how to spice up even the most boring of legal events. Sure glad we ended up at that same law function table years ago.

Thank you to my old firm for hiring me as a law student and then keeping me. My obnoxiousness may not be their style (they are very proper)—which in my new life definitely means

I'm doing something right—but I do thank all my mentors for all the training, and really, all the lawyers I worked with because every single one of them offered me gold nuggets aplenty.

Even bigger thanks to past clients, my funny and attentive workshop attendees (especially Bobby, Dave, Tommy, and Dan for starting us off) who dared to explore this idea and learn something new, and all the people I spoke with along the journey to developing the idea for this book. You are indeed the spark.

Thank you to the Scribe team who worked on the production of this book, especially my Publishing Manager, Erin Mellor, whose Zen-like, ever-sweet smile got this book to the white-and-black checkers; Jess LaGreca, whose patience and never-faltering creativity with my book cover should give her a Patience Award of the Year; and AJ Hendrickson, Mark Chait, and Emily Gindlesparger, for their work and guidance in editing the manuscript. Now that I think about it, they should probably all get the same award as Jess.

Much gratitude to Dan Nash, entrepreneur and real-life superhero, since he had to live with me during the process of writing this book. I'm grateful for his ideas and vision. As you might guess from even just seven pages that the average person reads of a book, I may not be the easiest person on the planet. Then again, I like a lot of sex and I'm a great cook—so how hard can I be? Asking for a friend.

But speaking of no-name friends, I'd like to say something to the millions of small business owners around the world who have at some point on the journey felt alone, defeated, crazy, whipped, tired...but still found a way to keep learning, innovating, and moving forward. It really is your tenacity and drive that fuels the fire of the entrepreneurial spirit. The best parts of the world would not exist without you. I honor you and can't put into words how much I appreciate you sharing this book with me. A book wouldn't be a book without a reader. The biggest thanks of all, therefore, goes to you.

DISCLOSURES AND DISCLAIMERS

BECAUSE THIS BOOK IS A GENERAL EDUCATIONAL INFORMATION PRODUCT, IT IS *NOT* A SUBSTITUTE FOR PROFESSIONAL LEGAL ADVICE BY AN ATTORNEY.

THIRD-PARTY INTELLECTUAL PROPERTY

All trademarks and service marks are the properties of their respective owners. All references to these properties are made solely for editorial purposes. Except for marks actually owned by the Author, no commercial claims are made to their use, and the Author is not affiliated with such marks in any way.

Unless otherwise expressly noted, none of the individuals or business entities mentioned herein has endorsed the contents of this book.

LIMITS OF LIABILITY AND DISCLAIMERS OF WARRANTIES

The materials in this book are provided "as is" and without warranties of any kind either express or implied. The Author disclaims all warranties, express or implied, including, but not limited to, implied warranties of merchantability and fitness for a particular purpose. The Author does not warrant that any defects will be corrected. The Author does not warrant or make any representations regarding the use or the results of the use of the materials in this book in terms of their correctness, accuracy, reliability, or otherwise. Applicable law may not allow the exclusion of implied warranties, so the above exclusion may not apply to you.

Under no circumstances, including, but not limited to, negligence, shall the Author be liable for any special or consequential damages that result from the use of, or the inability to use this book, even if the Author or an authorized representative has been advised of the possibility of such damages. Applicable law may not allow the limitation or exclusion of liability or incidental or consequential damages, so the above limitation or exclusion may not apply to you. In no event shall the Author's total liability to you for all damages, losses, and causes of action (whether in contract, tort, including but not limited to, negligence or otherwise) exceed the amount paid by you, if any, for this book.

You agree to hold the Author of this book, principals, agents, affiliates, and employees harmless from any and all liability for all claims for damages due to injuries, including attorney fees and costs, incurred by you or caused to third parties by you, arising out of the products, services, and activities discussed in this book, excepting only claims for gross negligence or intentional tort.

You agree that any and all claims for gross negligence or intentional tort shall be settled solely by confidential binding arbitration per the American Arbitration Association's commercial arbitration rules. Your claim cannot be aggregated with third party claims. All arbitration must occur in Christian County, Missouri, USA. Arbitration fees and costs shall be split equally, and you are solely responsible for your own lawyer fees.

Facts and information are believed to be accurate at the time they were placed in this book. Some names, dates, facts, locations, events, and other identifying features have been changed to protect the confidentiality, identity, and privacy rights of relevant parties. All data provided in this book is to be used for information purposes only. The information contained within is not intended to provide specific legal, financial, tax, physical or mental health advice, or any other advice whatsoever, for any individual or company and should not be relied upon in that regard. Products and services described are only offered in jurisdictions where they may be legally offered. Information provided is not all-inclusive, and is limited to information that is made available and such information should not be relied upon as all-inclusive or accurate.

For more information about this policy, please contact the Author at the email address listed in the *Copyright Notice* at the front of this book.

AFFILIATE COMPENSATION AND MATERIAL CONNECTIONS DISCLOSURE

This book may contain references to websites and information created and maintained by other individuals and organizations. The Author does not control or guarantee the accuracy, completeness, relevance, or timeliness of any information or privacy policies posted on these websites.

You should assume that all references to products and services in this book are made because material connections exist between the Author and the providers of the mentioned products and services ("Provider"). You should also assume that all website links within this book are affiliate links for (a) the Author, or (b) someone else who is an affiliate for the mentioned products and services (individually and collectively, the "Affiliate").

The Affiliate recommends products and services in this book based in part on a good faith belief that the purchase of such products or services will help readers in general.

The Affiliate has this good faith belief because (a) the Affiliate has tried the product or service mentioned prior to recommending it or (b) the Affiliate has researched the reputation of the Provider and has made the decision to recommend the Provider's products or services based on the Provider's history of providing these or other products or services.

The representations made by the Affiliate about products and services reflect the Affiliate's honest opinion based upon the facts known to the Affiliate at the time this book was published.

Because there is a material connection between the Affiliate and Providers of products or services mentioned in this book, you should always assume that the Affiliate may be biased because of the Affiliate's relationship with a Provider and/or because the Affiliate has received or will receive something of value from a Provider.

Perform your own due diligence before purchasing a product or service mentioned in this book.

The type of compensation received by the Affiliate may vary. In some instances, the Affiliate may receive complimentary products (such as a review copy), services, or money from a Provider prior to mentioning the Provider's products or services in this book.

In addition, the Affiliate may receive a monetary commission or non-monetary compensation when you take action by using a website link within this book. This includes, but is not limited to, when you purchase a product or service from a Provider after going to a website link contained in this book.

TIME AND MONETARY SAVINGS DISCLAIMERS

No Time or Monetary Savings Projections, Promises or Representations

For purposes of these disclaimers, the term "Author" refers individually and collectively to the author of this book and to the affiliate (if any) whose affiliate hyperlinks are referenced in this book.

You recognize and agree that the Author has made no implications, warranties, promises, suggestions, projections, representations or guarantees whatsoever to you about future prospects, time savings, or monetary savings, or that you will save any time or money, with respect to your purchase of this book and implementation of any information found within it. The Author has not authorized any such projection, promise, or representation by others.

Any time and monetary savings statements or examples are only estimates of what you *might* save. There is no assurance you will do as well as stated in any examples, or well at all. If you rely upon any figures provided, you must accept the entire risk of not doing as well as the information provided.

There is no assurance that any prior successes or past results as to time or monetary savings will apply, nor can any prior successes be used, as an indication of your future success or results from any of the information, content, or strategies. Any and all claims or representations as to savings are not to be considered as "average savings."

Testimonials and Examples

Testimonials and examples in this book are exceptional results, do not reflect the typical purchaser's experience, do not apply to the average person, and are not intended to represent or guarantee that anyone will achieve the same or similar results. Where specific time or monetary savings figures are used and attributed to a specific individual or business, that individual or business has saved that amount to the knowledge of the Author. There is no assurance that you will do as well using the same information or strategies. If you rely on the specific figures used, you must accept all the risk of not doing as well. The described experiences are atypical. Your results are likely to differ from those described in the testimonials and examples.

Your Success or Lack of It

Your success in using the information or strategies provided in this book depends on a variety of factors. The Author has no way of knowing how well you will do because she does not know you, your background, your work ethic, your dedication, your motivation, your desire, your attorney(s), the details of your legal matter(s), or your business skills or practices. Therefore, the Author does not guarantee or imply that you will do as well, or that you will have any time or monetary savings at all.

Purchase Price

Although the Author believes the price is fair for the value that you receive, you understand and agree that the purchase price for this book has been arbitrarily set by the Author or the vendor who sold you this book. This price bears no relationship to objective standards.

Due Diligence

You are advised to do your own due diligence when it comes to making any decisions. Use caution and seek the advice of qualified professionals before acting upon the contents of this book or any other information. You shall not consider any examples, documents, or other content in this book or otherwise provided by the Author to be the equivalent of legal advice, tax advice, or other professional advice.

The Author assumes no responsibility for any losses or damages resulting from your use of any link, information, or opportunity contained in this book or within any other information disclosed by the Author in any form whatsoever.

YOU SHOULD ALWAYS CONDUCT YOUR OWN INVESTIGATION (PERFORM DUE DILIGENCE) BEFORE BUYING PRODUCTS OR SERVICES FROM ANYONE. THIS INCLUDES PRODUCTS AND SERVICES SOLD VIA WEBSITE LINKS REFERENCED IN THIS BOOK.